CW00942964

Achieving Outstanding Classroom Support in Your Secondary School

Achieving Outstanding Classroom Support in Your Secondary School shows how secondary school teachers and other school staff can work with Teaching Assistants to ensure that classroom support is maximised and an optimum working relationship is developed.

Based on research taken directly from the classroom, all recommendations and guidelines explored in this book are based on the findings of those who have consulted Teaching Assistants about their work, in order to better understand the dynamics of classrooms where at least one of the adults present is supporting the other, directly or indirectly.

Topics studied include:

- Understanding the roles and responsibilities of the Teaching Assistant
- What the research tells us about Teaching Assistants
- How to plan before the lesson
- How to involve the Teaching Assistant in the lesson
- How to provide feedback and advocacy for the Teaching Assistant after the lesson

This accessible text provides a highly supportive framework to prompt teachers to be proactive and plan ahead for effective use of their Teaching Assistants in the classroom and will be of interest to all secondary teachers, SENCOs, heads of departments and school managers.

Jill Morgan is Senior Lecturer at the University of Wales Trinity Saint David, UK.

Cheryl Jones is Performance Specialist for SEN for the City and County of Swansea school improvement service and Lecturer at the University of Wales Trinity Saint David, UK.

Sioned Booth-Coates has been teaching for six years at secondary schools in the UK.

nasen is a professional membership association that supports all those who work with or care for children and young people with special and additional educational needs. Members include teachers, teaching assistants, support workers, other educationalists, students and parents.

nasen supports its members through policy documents, journals, its magazine *Special*, publications, professional development courses, regional networks and newsletters. Its website contains more current information such as responses to government consultations. **nasen's** published documents are held in very high regard both in the UK and internationally.

Other titles published in association with the National Association for Special Educational Needs (nasen):

Language for Learning in the Secondary School: A practical guide for supporting students with speech, language and communication needs
Sue Hayden and Emma Jordan
2012/pb: 978-0-415-61975-2

Using Playful Practice to Communicate with Special Children
Margaret Corke
2012/pb: 978-0-415-68767-6

The Equality Act for Educational Professionals: A simple guide to disability and inclusion in schools
Geraldine Hills
2012/pb: 978-0-415-68768-3

More Trouble with Maths: A teacher's complete guide to identifying and diagnosing mathematical difficulties
Steve Chinn
2012/pb: 978-0-415-67013-5

Dyslexia and Inclusion: Classroom approaches for assessment, teaching and learning, 2ed
Gavin Reid
2012/pb: 978-0-415-60758-2

Promoting and Delivering School-to-School Support for Special Educational Needs: A practical guide for SENCOs
Rita Cheminais
2013/pb 978-0-415-63370-3

Time to Talk: Implementing outstanding practice in speech, language and communication
Jean Gross
2013/pb: 978-0-415-63334-5

Curricula for Teaching Children and Young People with Severe or Profound and Multiple Learning Difficulties: Practical strategies for educational professionals
Peter Imray and Viv Hinchcliffe
2013/pb: 978-0-415-83847-4

Successfully Managing ADHD: A handbook for SENCOs and teachers
Fintan O'Regan
2014/pb: 978-0-415-59770-8

Brilliant Ideas for Using ICT in the Inclusive Classroom, 2ed
Sally McKeown and Angela McGlashon
2015/pb: 978-1-138-80902-4

Boosting Learning in the Primary Classroom: Occupational therapy strategies that really work with pupils
Sheilagh Blyth
2015/pb: 978-1-13-882678-6

Beating Bureaucracy in Special Educational Needs, 3ed
Jean Gross
2015/pb: 978-1-138-89171-5

Transforming Reading Skills in the Secondary School: Simple strategies for improving literacy
Pat Guy
2015/pb: 978-1-138-89272-9

Supporting Children with Speech and Language Difficulties, 2ed
Cathy Allenby, Judith Fearon-Wilson, Sally Merrison and Elizabeth Morling
2015/pb: 978-1-138-85511-3

Supporting Children with Dyspraxia and Motor Co-ordination Difficulties, 2ed
Susan Coulter, Lesley Kynman, Elizabeth Morling, Rob Grayson and Jill Wing
2015/pb: 978-1-138-85507-6

Developing Memory Skills in the Primary Classroom: A complete programme for all
Gill Davies
2015/pb: 978-1-138-89262-0

Language for Learning in the Primary School: A practical guide for supporting pupils with language and communication difficulties across the curriculum, 2ed
Sue Hayden and Emma Jordan
2015/pb: 978-1-138-89862-2

Supporting Children with Autistic Spectrum Disorders, 2ed
Elizabeth Morling and Colleen O'Connell
2016/pb: 978-1-138-85514-4

Understanding and Supporting Pupils with Moderate Learning Difficulties in the Secondary School: A practical guide
Rachael Hayes and Pippa Whittaker
2016/pb: 978-1-138-01910-2

Assessing Children with Specific Learning Difficulties: A teacher's practical guide
Gavin Reid, Gad Elbeheri and John Everatt
2016/pb: 978-0-415-67027-2

Supporting Children with Down's Syndrome, 2ed
Lisa Bentley, Ruth Dance, Elizabeth Morling, Susan Miller and Susan Wong
2016/pb: 978-1-138-91485-8

Provision Mapping and the SEND Code of Practice: Making it work in primary, secondary and special schools, 2ed
Anne Massey
2016/pb: 978-1-138-90707-2

Supporting Children with Medical Conditions, 2ed
Susan Coulter, Lesley Kynman, Elizabeth Morling, Francesca Murray, Jill Wing and Rob Grayson
2016/pb: 978-1-13-891491-9

Achieving Outstanding Classroom Support in Your Secondary School: Tried and tested strategies for teachers and SENCOs
Jill Morgan, Cheryl Jones, Sioned Booth-Coates
2016/pb: 978-1-138-83373-9

Achieving Outstanding Classroom Support in Your Secondary School

Tried and tested strategies for teachers and SENCOs

Jill Morgan, Cheryl Jones and Sioned Booth-Coates

Taylor & Francis Group

LONDON AND NEW YORK

Helping Everyone Achieve

First published 2016
by Routledge
2 Park Square, Milton Park, Abingdon, Oxon OX14 4RN

and by Routledge
711 Third Avenue, New York, NY 10017

Routledge is an imprint of the Taylor & Francis Group, an informa business

© 2016 J. Morgan, C. Jones and S. Booth-Coates

The right of J. Morgan, C. Jones and S. Booth-Coates to be identified as authors of this work has been asserted by them in accordance with sections 77 and 78 of the Copyright, Designs and Patents Act 1988.

All rights reserved. The purchase of this copyright material confers the right on the purchasing institution to photocopy pages which bear the photocopy icon and copyright line at the bottom of the page. No other part of this publication may be reproduced, stored in a retrieval system, or transmitted in any form or by any means, electronic, mechanical, photocopying, recording or otherwise, without prior permission in writing from the publisher.

Trademark notice: Product or corporate names may be trademarks or registered trademarks, and are used only for identification and explanation without intent to infringe.

British Library Cataloguing in Publication Data
A catalogue record for this book is available from the British Library

Library of Congress Cataloging-in-Publication Data
Morgan, Jill, 1956–
Achieving outstanding classroom support in your secondary school : tried and tested strategies for teachers and SENCOs / Jill Morgan, Cheryl Jones and Sioned Booth-Coates.
pages cm
1. Teachers' assistants. 2. Classroom management. I. Jones, Cheryl. II. Booth-Coates, Sioned. III. Title.
LB2844.1.A8M648 2016
371.14'124--dc23
2015020096

ISBN: 978-1-138-83372-2 (hbk)
ISBN: 978-1-138-83373-9 (pbk)
ISBN: 978-1-315-73528-3 (ebk)

Typeset in Sabon and Gill Sans
by Saxon Graphics Ltd, Derby
Printed in Great Britain by Ashford Colour Press Ltd.

We dedicate this book to family, friends and colleagues who have freely shared their ideas and opinions, and listened to ours over the many years we have been working for and with Teaching Assistants.

Contents

Preface

Teaching Assistants (under a variety of titles) have been a feature of our classrooms for decades, but relatively few books have been written about them and their work, for those who have the most direct and daily responsibility for overseeing that work: teachers and SENCOs. Decisions about TA deployment may rest initially with the school leadership, but once those decisions are made, it is the teachers and SENCOs who need practical advice on how to work directly – and most effectively – with support staff in classrooms. What has been written to date has largely targeted primary school settings. This book specifically addresses the supervision of TAs' work in secondary school settings, in recognition of the very different organisational structures which make collaborative work between teachers/SENCOs and TAs more challenging.

Subsequent to the 2003 National Agreement on raising standards and tackling teacher workload, the number of TAs working in our schools increased dramatically. However, publications relating to TAs' work has remained largely in the academic domain rather than entering the stream of professional literature. And there has been a great deal published, with variations on the same themes: the necessity of defining and assigning appropriate roles for TAs, the need to provide adequate training for those roles, the associated need for teachers to be better prepared to work with TAs, time for teachers and TAs to plan and debrief. *Plus ça change*. But change is in the air. Beginning with the *Deployment and Impact of Support Staff* (DISS), a series of research projects (largely from London University's Institute of Education) have drilled down through system-wide school issues relating to TAs, to the details of their everyday interactions with students. The bad news of the DISS findings – that students supported by TAs may make less progress than similar students who receive no support – is being replaced by knowledge that should allow us to reverse that trend.

More targeted training for TAs would be the subject of another book and will take time to filter into the school system. Here we address the needs of teachers and SENCOs, and how they can work with Teaching Assistants to ensure that the support provided in the classroom is maximally effective, and that a positive working relationship is developed between the adults who work together in the classroom.

This book is a straightforward, easy-to-use guide for secondary school teachers and SENCOs as the staff members who have primary contact with and daily responsibility for TAs. They also have the task of providing ongoing supervision (monitoring, assessment of skills, meeting training needs, etc.). More specifically the objectives for this book include:

- providing a framework to prompt teachers to be proactive and plan ahead for effective use of TAs in their classrooms;
- providing practical suggestions for how classroom support by TAs can best be used;
- providing planning sheets and other outline documentation to facilitate the development of effective working relationships between teachers and the TAs who support learning and teaching in their classrooms.

This book is structured in terms of *Before, During* and *After* so that practical strategies are presented for planning ahead, actually working with the TA, and follow-up. But all the strategies and suggestions are firmly based on research and the experience of those who have worked in secondary schools, including teachers and TAs themselves.

Acknowledgements

We would like to acknowledge schools, teachers, Teaching Assistants and SENCOs of the City & County of Swansea for their willing participation in our research, helping us to better understand the issues relating to the deployment and impact of support staff in secondary school settings.

We would also like to thank the editorial team at Routledge for their encouragement and support.

Abbreviations

ALN	Additional Learning Needs
CA	Classroom Assistant (Scotland, Ireland)
DfE	Department for Education
DfES	Department for Education and Science
DISS	Deployment and Impact of Support Staff
EHCP	Education and Health Care Plan
ESEA	Elementary and Secondary Education Act
HLTA	Higher Level Teaching Assistant
IDEA	Individuals with Disabilities Education Act
IEP	Individual Education Plan
NCLB	No Child Left Behind
PPA time	Preparation, Planning and Assessment time
SEN	Special Educational Needs
SENCO	Special Educational Needs Coordinator
SOW	Scheme of Work
TA	Teaching Assistant

Introduction

This is a book about classroom support – what it can look like, and how it can be most effective in your classroom. If you are a secondary school teacher or SENCO working with TAs or other classroom support staff in a secondary school, this book is for you. It can be used as a type of self-study guide, or it could be used as the basis of a faculty-based or whole-school in-service. And as the effectiveness of TAs' work affects the whole school, it could also provide a template for a school improvement initiative.

We recognise that there are many ways in which secondary schools operate differently from primary schools, and so in this book we offer insights and advice appropriate to the dynamics of the way your classrooms most likely work, and the staffing patterns that are more typical of secondary than of primary school settings. Decisions about these staffing patterns will already have been made by your school's senior management team, and if you are a SENCO, you may have some part in those decisions. But as a subject teacher, your decision-making most likely only relates to your own classroom and how you will work with whoever has been assigned to support the students who come there. This book is designed to help you with those decisions, so that you can work most effectively, for the benefit of your students.

First we would like to reminisce a little about our own experiences of working with TAs and other support staff (we'll call them TAs for ease of reading). You may find yourself nodding or smiling as you read and find similarities with your own experience; or you may be new to the teaching profession or have little experience of working with TAs. Whichever is the case, as you read these reminiscences, take the time to consider the recurring themes in them, and see how they resonate with your own experience.

The teacher's perspective (Sioned Booth-Coates)

I first realised I wanted to work in education and specifically SEN at 14 when I volunteered on a weekly basis at a special school in North Wales – helping in after-school clubs, holidays to Disneyland Paris (that was a tough one!) and many Duke of Edinburgh expeditions. My degree was drama and psychology and I purposely chose modules relating to education and SEN throughout my three years (individual differences, challenging behaviour, autism and dyslexia), although my PGCE subjects were drama and English.

I've been teaching for five years now and have taught pupils with SEN/ALN in drama, music and English, with many of the pupils bringing their TA support with them. It's been intriguing to see different TAs' strengths within differing subjects even with the same student. Currently I'm head of psychology and deputy head of sixth form as well as teaching English at a Welsh comprehensive. I recently completed a course on the SEN Code of Practice where the presenter discussed research that had been completed into the effectiveness of TAs in primary schools. The findings from the primary schools were 'glowing' and I wanted to discover whether the same was true in the secondary sector. I think there's so much we don't know about TAs and the ways they work.

The SENCO's perspective (Jayne Smith)

My first teaching post in 1980 was in Soho in a tiny primary school populated by mostly Chinese and Italian children. In my first class were 21 students aged 7–9 plus one 14-year-old boy – who was quite strange. I worried about him and his influence on the other pupils because he loved looking in all the 'adult' shop windows on his way to school. However, I told myself that everything would be alright – because he had a Teaching Assistant.

New to the school and to teaching, with only teaching practice behind me, no one had mentioned Teaching Assistants, or special needs, and now I come to think of it, no one ever did. Looking back, the assistant and I must have communicated through telepathy, probably having only one very brief conversation a week about her pupil. I didn't worry about him, though, or her. They seemed to get on great with the lessons and were very happy. If anyone else had any concerns, I wasn't told about them – and I didn't really think it was my business to ask!

I worked in various primary schools in London and then in Wales, with no TAs. Even with a Year 3/4 special needs class of 17 pupils – no TAs. But in 1999 I joined a specialist teaching facility (STF) in a secondary school with 20+ pupils, one other teacher and six TAs, and in 2000 I became head of the STF, and I was suddenly in charge of all these people.

Although there was a high turnover of TAs, a core of three mature ladies (mothers) stayed on, and they were worth their weight in gold. Although not trained in special needs or speech and language difficulties, they had common sense, a fierce loyalty to the STF and to the pupils' wellbeing and safety. They did everything I asked them to do without hesitation or drama. We worked as a team. We were all friends and equals. We all knew what we were doing. We all belonged to the STF.

Since then, I was put in charge of another eight TAs who were allocated to individual pupils in mainstream, then a new build for the STF brought additional pupils with another six TAs and a new teacher, complicated by a new policy of accepting pupils with severe behaviour/mental health problems.

But I've noticed that the difference between the 'mainstream' TAs and the 'STF TAs' is quite profound. There are also quite distinct differences between the younger and the more experienced TAs. They're a very diverse group. They told me they didn't know what they were supposed to be doing, so our meetings became problem-solving meetings and the mainstream TAs were able to resolve some issues and adopt some of the STF routines. There's a frustration among TAs that they are not valued by the senior management of the school. There's been a high absenteeism too; having to cover break- and lunchtime duties as well as being in the classroom all day can be stressful and quite frankly exhausting.

There are some definite positives, though:

- The TAs have struck up good friendships – they enjoy seeing each other after school and on the weekends.
- One of the TAs was seen during a recent inspection and received a glowing verbal report, which reflected well on us all.
- I was pleased in my recent observations of 'my' TAs who generally supported pupils very well and our approach to make the pupils independent learners shone through.

So life continues challenging, but there are definitely bright spots, and I think we're getting there.

The local authority perspective (Cheryl Jones)

Classroom support! What's that?

My experience as a mainstream teacher started in the days before Teaching Assistants, the days before the National Curriculum and the days when the cane was an accepted way to discipline pupils! So 'support' was not a widely used term! Young teachers such as myself just got on with it as best we could. In general, pupils with learning difficulties or anything different to the norm were largely ignored and expectations were low.

I started out as a secondary school teacher, and was taken to my first class of 15-year-olds with the words, 'Just keep them in, don't worry about what you teach them!' I'd not heard of data, outcomes or assessments, I just tried my best. If the pupil didn't succeed, then I tried another way. No one supported me or gave me any strategies to try. It would have been wonderful to have any kind of support!

Moving on from the 1970s and 1980s I became a support teacher, taking groups out of mainstream classes. I don't know whether the teachers wondered who I was or what I did with the pupils, but we worked out of the classroom, then after about an hour returned – enough time to give the mainstream teacher a rest from the more challenging pupils. I never planned with anyone and was left to my own devices. The children did make progress, however, no one asked me how I did it!

Then Teaching Assistants arrived! Not just 'mums' army' but ladies (predominantly) to support the teacher. As a SENCO in a mainstream primary, I came to appreciate and rely on my (I repeat, 'my' – we were very territorial) Teaching Assistants. They supported the pupils as well as myself, reinforcing concepts learned and sometimes photocopying in those days.

Coming up to the present time, working for the local authority, my perspective on classroom support is quite different from my early experience. The most effective classroom support I have seen is where it is planned, discussed and evaluated. The Teaching Assistants are involved and monitor progress alongside the teacher; they are trained and know their role.

In my role as adviser and trainer of TAs, my key message is that all classroom support should endeavour to make the pupils independent not dependent – trained, targeted support rather than general support.

The higher education perspective (Jill Morgan)

I'm a teacher – well I used to be because I now work in higher education, and the people I now teach are either working in classrooms or hoping to, as I run a Foundation Degree in Learning Support for TAs. But I clearly remember my own early experiences of Teaching Assistants (known ironically as non-teaching staff in those days). I'd moved from Buckinghamshire schools, where the only learning support was the remedial reading teacher (who withdrew pupils from the classroom for about an hour a day), to London, where I did supply work for the ILEA and where it felt as if I were surrounded by other adults as well as pupils in the classroom. From being in sole charge of the classroom, with no witnesses to my competence (or incompetence) as a teacher – except the pupils, of course – I had to learn to work alongside and manage a variety of adults as well as pupils.

I remember the first day in a particular primary school where I worked early on as a supply teacher. No sooner had I settled the class on the carpet, to talk about what we were going to do for the day, when someone I didn't know popped her head around the door and with a cheery 'I'll take my group now' promptly disappeared along with four (or was it five?) pupils and their recorders. Nothing quite so well designed to undermine your authority, as having to ask the remainder of the class, 'So who was that? And where have those children gone? Do you know when they'll be back?' Fortunately this was a class who were willing to help an ignorant supply teacher, rather than taking advantage of her. They reassured me that the group would only be gone for about 25 minutes (though there was some discussion about the timing) and then the second group would leave for about the same time. So in the space of five minutes I had to revise my plans for the day for the second time, to include the future leavers as well as the current ones, and returned to discussing the day's topic with the class. However, not five minutes later, another head popped around the door. This time I was better prepared and managed to ask her who she was, who she was taking, why, and for how long. Jean. Group of five. Cookery. About three-quarters of an hour. By now I'm on plan C, and looking forward to a bit of group work myself. When another stranger entered the room unannounced, I was prepared to offer her half of my remaining pupils, but she seemed quite shocked at the suggestion, as if it were beneath her to deal with children. 'I've just come to sharpen your pencils!' And indeed, as I discovered later in the staff room, she did think it beneath her dignity to deal directly with the children, except to occasionally hear them read – she made that very clear, and all of the teachers heard and obeyed!

These early experiences have been much supplemented over the years by my work with TAs and teachers outside their classrooms as much as inside, as I've provided training and workshops, and now the Foundation Degree. I think we've come a long way from those early days, with many TAs better prepared for their roles, but I fear that many teachers are still as unprepared as I was all those years ago.

And the TA perspective?

What is missing from these reminiscences of course is the TA's perspective, but you will hear the voice of TAs all through the remaining chapters of the book, as we make suggestions based on the research about and with TAs. We'll be basing our recommendations and guidelines on the findings of those who have consulted TAs about their work, in order to better understand the dynamics of classrooms where more than one adult is present and one of those is supporting the other, directly or indirectly.

Although this book is intended as a practical guide, it is very much based on research – some of it our own, some conducted by others. We have included a bibliography at the back of the book, so that you can extend your reading if that is of interest to you, but in the first chapter of the book we have included some excerpts from the research – a synopsis to support the practical suggestions that follow so you can have confidence that what we are suggesting is based on real classrooms where people like yourself and your support staff work. These are not just our suggestions – we are the messengers relaying the thoughts and ideas of TAs and the students they work with.

You may be interested to know that the findings of research in the UK are mirrored by research in the United States and other countries – that our situation is not unique, but that the challenges (and potential solutions) of working with other adults in the classroom are replicated in classrooms in many other parts of the world. Researchers in the United States, for example, have commented on:

- The increasingly complex and sophisticated roles assigned to TAs – from being non-teaching staff in primary schools to the current levels of involvement with direct instructional responsibilities.
- Our over-reliance on TAs to support students with special or additional learning needs and the school system that is trying to provide for them.
- The risks we take in assigning the most needy students to the members of staff who may be the least qualified to help them, as regards subject knowledge and teaching skills.
- The need for teachers to be better prepared (through initial teacher education programmes) to work in collaboration with support staff.

These are issues that have been exercising the minds of practitioners and academics for decades. Although we cannot claim to have resolved them, this book will provide you with practical advice on how you can make best use of this valuable resource we refer to as Teaching Assistants, based on our own joint experiences of working with teachers and TAs, and on research evidence.

Before you launch into the main body of the book – although we know you have probably already dipped in to check how useful this book is going to be for you – it might be useful to reflect on your experiences of and attitudes towards classroom support. We have provided a pro forma for this, in the form of an audit on pages 6–7. Recognising that you may not wish to write on the book, and that these are private reflections, you can – without infringing copyright – photocopy the audit pages *for your own use*.

You may of course have not just one but several TAs who pass through your classroom during the course of the week, supporting a variety of student needs, and your feelings about TAs may differ according to which one of the many you focus on. But even that can tell you a lot about effective classroom support, as you reflect on the differences and things you might like to see changed.

Having reflected on your attitude and practice, the question which arises now is '*So what?*' What will you do about it? Is it easier to stop here and not move on? But before you do that we would like to take you back to one of the questions on the first page of the audit: *What is it that I really want from support staff?*

This should not just be a question of what you want a TA to *do* (e.g. make sure the student has the necessary resources, leave you a note about the student's progress at the end of the lesson). It is a deeper question of how you really see her role. (We refer to TAs as 'she' to avoid the awkwardness of 'he/she' and in line with the consistent research findings that over 90% of TAs in the UK, and elsewhere, are women.)

Is she really just a child-minder? (Without her present the student is a nuisance, disrupting your teaching and getting nothing done; when she's there the disruption ceases – or at least she takes it out of the classroom if it occurs – and at least the student gets something done.)

Or is she to be a contributing member of the instructional team?

As you have decided to read this book, we assume that the latter is the case – that you want something better from the TA's presence than just child-minding, and that you want to increase your own skills and understanding of how two adults can work together effectively. We will be reminding you of this question regularly throughout the book, as the actions you take should be based on this question as a matter of principle rather than just a matter of task-assignment.

Some of the questions included in the audit highlight some entrenched (and not very positive) attitudes to Teaching Assistants. Let's look at an example we have observed in a school.

This is a science lesson in a secondary school. Year 9 students enter and find their seats. The class includes seven students identified as having SEN and one student who has a statement for speech, language and communication difficulties. Two young Teaching Assistants enter and sit at the back of the classroom to support some of the students. The teacher starts the lesson. Most of the students are engaged, although the two TAs are whispering at the back. The teacher stops the lesson to tell the TAs to be quiet, then the lesson continues.

At the end of the lesson the students leave along with the two TAs and the teacher prepares for the next class to arrive.

When we ask the teacher about what the TAs were doing during the class, the teacher's response is 'I don't know what they're doing here. What use are they? They just sit and whisper in the back of my class. Employ more teachers – that's what the kids need!'

Classroom support: self-audit

Ask yourself:

Do I generally like to work as part of a team? Or do I prefer to work alone and independently?

When I was told that I would have TA support in some of my classes, was I relieved? Or disappointed?

What was the source of that relief (or disappointment)? Why did I feel that way? And what does that say about my attitude towards TAs and their usefulness in my classroom?

What is it that I really want from support staff?

If I had total control over the support provided to the students I teach, I would...

The set of statements on the following page was presented to TAs as part of a research study we carried out. You will find a summary of their responses in the next chapter. Here we have adapted the statements to your perspective as a teacher. Tick one of the boxes to the right of the statements, then consider what you might need to focus on to increase the effectiveness of your work with the TA, and look out for practical guidance on that area as you read through the remainder of the book.

© 2016, *Achieving Outstanding Classroom Support in Your Secondary School*, J. Morgan, C. Jones and S. Booth-Coates, Routledge

Statement	Tick one
I know the strengths and skills of the TAs who work in my classroom	☐ Definitely ☐ To some extent ☐ Not at all
I make use of the TAs' strengths and skills	☐ Definitely ☐ To some extent ☐ Not at all
I like the TAs to use their initiative when working with the students	☐ Definitely ☐ To some extent ☐ Not at all
I value TAs' opinions on the individual students they support	☐ Definitely ☐ To some extent ☐ Not at all
The TA and I are partners in supporting children's learning	☐ Definitely ☐ To some extent ☐ Not at all
I encourage the TAs to attend training and take up professional development opportunities	☐ Definitely ☐ To some extent ☐ Not at all
I try to support the TAs when they come to work in my classroom	☐ Definitely ☐ To some extent ☐ Not at all
I value the work that TAs do in our school	☐ Definitely ☐ To some extent ☐ Not at all
I think TAs' work in the school has a positive impact on children's learning	☐ Definitely ☐ To some extent ☐ Not at all

© 2016, *Achieving Outstanding Classroom Support in Your Secondary School*, J. Morgan, C. Jones and S. Booth-Coates, Routledge

This is a recent example from an otherwise competent teacher. So the question we would pose is: *Who is losing out in that lesson?*

The students? Very definitely, yes.

The students with additional needs may need scaffolding to access the lesson. The language that the teacher was using may have been too complicated for them to process. The whispering was no doubt the TAs trying to simplify the language and tasks. There may have also been other students in the class who would have benefitted from the TAs' input to provide assurance for their written work – if the TAs had been allowed to move around the room. So a number of the students may have been losing out in terms of not getting the full support they needed.

Was the teacher losing out? Absolutely.

The TAs could have provided extra support in delivering the lesson – checking that the material was accessible to students identified as having additional needs. They could have worked with groups and simplified the instructions for the students with Speech Language and Communication Difficulties (SLCD) in order to ensure they could engage with the material. Other forms of differentiated work could have been provided for other students and the TAs could have been assigned to support this. At the conclusion of the lesson, the teacher could have asked for feedback from the TAs on the progress of the students in order to prepare for the next lesson.

And lastly, did the TAs lose out? Yes, again.

The TAs could have been an essential and integral part of the lesson in ensuring all students understood the instructions. They could have supported both teacher and students in improving standards. However, as they were not included in any discussion with the teacher, they most likely left feeling unvalued and not really needed or involved in the lesson. They would certainly have sensed the teacher's irritation and hostility.

There is so much that could have been achieved in that lesson that was missed! Therefore the question from the audit really is key: *What is it that you want from your TAs?*

On p. 9 you will find a simple pro forma for developing an action plan in relation to your work with TAs, which you can begin to use now in response to the self-audit. Or you may prefer to complete it as you work your way through the chapters of the book.

The benefits and drawbacks of Teaching Assistants

In a 2002 survey of teachers (see Neill (2002) in the Bibliography) three out of four teachers saw the most significant benefit of TA support as providing additional support for groups or individual students. Fewer than one in ten teachers referred to the benefits of working in partnership with another adult, or even reduction of a teacher's workload. However, two out of three the teachers surveyed could identify drawbacks to working with TAs, the most common being that TAs' skills, experience or qualifications varied considerably. The next most commonly cited drawbacks related to the fact that they (the teachers) felt they lacked the skills to manage or supervise TAs, and the lack of time available for them to meet with TAs. The report's author did not interpret these responses as reluctance to work with TAs generally.

Action plan

Action	How to achieve it Outline steps	Who will help me?	Date achieved
1.			
2.			
3.			
4.			

© 2016, *Achieving Outstanding Classroom Support in Your Secondary School*, J. Morgan, C. Jones and S. Booth-Coates, Routledge

The remainder of the book is structured as follows.

We start with a chapter on *differentiation* as a reminder of why we really have TAs in our classrooms. The wide variety of student needs in any given year group requires that we differentiate what we offer, in a variety of different ways. TAs have largely been employed on this basis, with *support* being one of the forms of differentiating the work of teaching.

The next chapter looks at the research relating to the work of TAs. This includes research carried out in secondary schools in South Wales, but that is set in the larger context of research carried out in England and Wales (and elsewhere), particularly the most recent research and guidance which provides us with a solid base of evidence about the work and impact of TAs. In 2009 the Audit Commission discussed the difficulties faced by schools when having to decide whether to employ additional teachers or TAs, because of the lack of solid evidence on the cost effectiveness of employing TAs. They recommended that stakeholders should work towards increasing the evidence base for TA effectiveness and impact. This is what we report on in Chapter 2 – the incremental understanding of TAs' contribution to classrooms, gained through empirical research.

The following three chapters form the practical core of the book. Framed in terms of *before, during* and *after*, they consider how teachers and SENCOs can plan for, work with and work for TAs to enhance their effectiveness. As we have stated, this is an expectation of all teachers, even though it may not have formed part of initial or subsequent training content. Thus we have been very specific in the suggestions we make, with many of the ideas being very straightforward and easy to implement, and requiring relatively little time. Other suggestions of course will require a greater time commitment and effort, but can be implemented incrementally. The suggestions are aimed mainly at teachers, but in each of these chapters we include supporting ideas and suggestions which would fall more naturally to the SENCO.

And lastly we summarise and consider general themes which have occurred through the book. We have also included:

- an extensive bibliography (with many of the items freely available online)
- a list of useful websites and other sources of relevant information
- *Top tips* for working with students with a variety of difficulties, such as dyslexia, and speech, language and communication difficulties. These can be photocopied for your TAs as appropriate. And although being a teenager is not a legal category of difficulty, because of the unique nature of this group of students, we have also included *Top tips* for working with teens.

So we hope that you find this an informative and practical book which will serve to enhance both the effectiveness of the work of your TA and your own effectiveness as a teacher or SENCO. And lastly, we have indeed included a TA's perspective – Anita Wooltorton's blog.

A 2010 report from Ofsted (the government inspectorate for schools in England) suggested that effective deployment of support staff is essentially a skill: "The quality of support for teaching and learning depend[s] very much on teachers' ability to manage and evaluate the effectiveness of members of the workforce" although the report also concedes: "it is a considerable challenge for teachers to direct the work of additional adults in the classroom" (Ofsted, 2010, p. 10).

Bibliography

Fox, G. (2007) *A Handbook for Learning Support Assistants: Teachers and Assistants Working Together.* Abingdon: Routledge.

Neill, S.R.St.J. (2002) *Teaching Assistants: A Survey Analysed for the National Union of Teachers.* Warwick: University of Warwick Institute of Education, Teacher Research & Development Unit. Available at: www.leeds.ac.uk/educol/documents/151758.doc (accessed 20.4.15)

Ofsted (2010) *Workforce Reform in Schools: Has it Made a difference? An Evaluation of Changes made to the School Workforce 2003–2009.* London: Ofsted.

Packer, N. and Beere, J. (2014) *The Perfect SENCO.* Carmarthen: Independent Thinking Press.

Watkinson, A. (2003) *Managing Teaching Assistants: A Guide for Headteachers, Managers and Teachers.* London: Routledge.

Roles and responsibilities

We have acknowledged already that working with TAs may not have been something you anticipated when you first trained as a teacher. You chose this profession no doubt because you wanted to work with young people. Even if you gained your teaching qualification fairly recently, as we have already acknowledged, your training may not have addressed working with and directing the work of TAs. But as we will discuss, working in collaboration with support staff is clearly one of the expectations of teachers, as it appears in the standards for qualified teachers in all regions of the UK. Effective deployment is also an aspect of schools in which inspectorates are taking an increased interest, further emphasising the need for teachers to add the skills associated with this responsibility to their repertoire. And as the subsequent chapters of the book make clear, there is an associated skill set and a range of actions that can be taken when carrying out this responsibility.

So we begin this chapter with a brief overview of the regulatory mandates for teachers working with TAs, and then consider some of the main principles of differentiation as the basis for employment of TAs. Lastly we consider some of the characteristics of this group of employees and the implications for classroom practice.

Requirements across the UK

In all four regions of the UK, regulations relating to both special and mainstream education address the question of TAs and the teacher's responsibility to actively work with them. The SEND Code of Practice (DfE, 2015) for England states that:

> Teachers are responsible and accountable for the progress and development of the pupils in their class, including where pupils access support from teaching assistants or specialist staff.

Implicit in this statement is the word 'all' – teachers are responsible and accountable for *all* the pupils in their class. And not simply responsible in a general sense, but responsible for their progress and development. It could be argued that teachers delegate some of this responsibility to TAs. However, the 2011 general Teachers' Standards in England (DfE, 2011) lists as part of a teacher's 'wider professional responsibilities':

- develop effective professional relationships with colleagues, knowing how and when to draw on advice and specialist support and
- deploy support staff effectively.

As we discuss throughout the course of this book, effective deployment does not mean handing over a student to the sole charge of a TA and expecting the TA to take care of the student's needs. The deployment of TAs and the type of work they undertake clearly needs to be a joint venture.

Published teacher standards from the other regions of the UK also make reference to working with other adults in the classroom, including support staff.

In Wales, the guidance for Qualified Teacher Status (QTS) (DCELLS, 2009) provides extensive detail of the many ways in which teachers are expected to work with TAs, including: "recognise and understand the contribution provided by and needed from support staff ... in the learning process".

Teachers must also "understand how other adults ... can contribute to teaching and learning and how teachers can use this contribution as a resource. This understanding assumes awareness of other colleagues' roles and how a teacher's responsibilities relate to and complement those of others."

To gain QTS, trainees must "demonstrate that they take part in, and contribute to, teaching teams ... [and] plan for the deployment of additional adults who support learning in children and young people".

In Scotland the *Mandatory Requirements for Registration with the General Teaching Council for Scotland* (General Teaching Council for Scotland, 2012) include:

> create and sustain appropriate working relationships with all staff ... to support learning and wellbeing, taking a lead role when appropriate and work collaboratively to contribute to the professional learning and development of colleagues, through offering support and constructive advice and through disseminating experience and expertise, seeking opportunities to lead learning.

This requirement clearly includes the provision of training of TAs. The General Teaching Council for Northern Ireland's 2011 document *Teaching: The Reflective Profession* states that:

> Teachers will deploy, organise and guide the work of other adults to support pupils' learning, when appropriate.

At initial training stage they are required only to gain an understanding of the "potential benefits arising from the deployment of other adults to support learning". However, even during induction they must identify roles and responsibilities of additional adults who work in the classroom, and also "deploy them effectively to help personalise pupils' learning and plan and organise how they are to support learning".

Similarly the school inspectorates of each of the regions make clear statements about the needs for teachers to engage in working with TAs. The Education and Training Inspectorate in Northern Ireland states that teachers are responsible for managing and organising the day-to-day work of Classroom Assistants (CAs) who support students with special needs in their classrooms. Unfortunately, a 2005–6 report on the effective use of CAs noted that very few of the schools inspected provided guidance for teachers in how to carry out this role. Likewise few teachers reported having received training or advice from their schools on how to manage CAs' work.

In Wales, 2010 guidance from Estyn on school inspections, under the heading of Good Resource Management, specifies:

> The school deploys teaching and support staff well and they have the knowledge and expertise to cover all aspects of the school's curriculum.

In Scotland, the publication *How Good is Our School?* (HMIe, 2007) provides quality indicators for schools, among them *Staff Deployment and Teamwork*. Illustrating a Level 5 school (on a

6-point scale) one of the statements reads: "Our staff team is deployed effectively to meet learners' needs and improve provision. Staff such as ... classroom assistants work in classrooms and contribute effectively to our learners' progress."

These are unequivocal and far-reaching statements of the expectations of teachers.

As a SENCO...

There is a real need to see the TA as a learner or trainee as well as a colleague. This book is not just about getting teacher and TAs together in order to create a more friendly, collegial atmosphere in the school – it is about increasing the overall effectiveness of *all* staff who are involved in the teaching and learning process that is central to the school's purpose. Some of the TAs in your school will have received a certain level of training and preparation for their work, but realistically much of the work they do is of a highly specialised nature and requires proper teaching skills. This may be controversial, from a number of perspectives:

- They do not have the professional status of a teacher, because they have not received the appropriate professional preparation and accreditation.
- They are not paid at the same level as professional teaching staff, so they should not be required to operate at the same level of expertise.

So there are those who say that TAs should not be 'teaching'. Nevertheless, within the limits of their job description and despite their non-professional status, their assignments so often relate to the enhancement of learning for students who struggle. The knowledge and skills required to carry out this work successfully are significant. We would go so far as to say that many teachers do not have a clear understanding of the needs of students who struggle, particularly in secondary schools where the emphasis is on teachers' subject content knowledge. So how can we expect TAs to act in a teaching capacity on behalf of the teacher without proper preparation? If schools are to continue to rely on TAs – particularly for students whose needs are different from the majority of the class – schools need to make the proper investment in their ongoing training. As a SENCO you may be best placed to advocate for this training, especially as local need will be quite specific, so training needs to be tailored according to those needs and the current skills and knowledge of your TAs.

A 2007 report by Estyn states: "The significant increase in support staff numbers means that senior teachers find it time-consuming to organise and deploy these staff."

This has been a very real concern for some years now in schools, but the Estyn report also offered reassurance: "there is evidence that TAs who are suitably qualified and supervised will make a difference to student achievement". This is encouraging, but it also highlights the importance of the twin needs of support staff: relevant training and supervision.

We cannot over-emphasise the above point. In the next chapter we look at the research relating to TAs, some of which indicates that TAs' work is not as impactful as we would like. But it should be no surprise if we weigh the responsibilities they are given against the preparation they receive for those responsibilities. We repeat the question that we first asked in the Introduction: *What is it that you want from your TA?* If you want competence commensurate with the demands of her work assignments, someone must take the necessary steps to ensure she has the necessary skills.

Working together

You may recall from your initial training or subsequent study the work of theorists such as Lev Vygotsky and Jerome Bruner, who viewed learning from a social constructivist perspective: that learning is a process of making sense of the world, and this sense-making is enhanced through interactions with others. Their theories largely related to children's early learning but some of the underlying principles offer food for thought in relation to teachers' work with TAs:

1. **Learning is a process of interaction between the known and the unknown, or what is yet to be learned.**

   In relation to teachers and TAs: this highlights how important it is for the learner (in this case the TA) to be aware of what she already knows; the need for the teacher to find out what the TA already knows prior to introducing new skills or knowledge (we suggest a skills audit later in the book); and the real need for the teacher to make links for the TA between what she already knows and the new information.

2. **Learning is a social process, where interaction with others allows for the sharing of knowledge and understanding.**

   In relation to teachers and TAs: this highlights the idea that meaningful learning is more likely to occur when deliberate action is taken, focusing on a topic or area of joint interest and importance; merely being present as an observer in the classroom is a poor substitute for deliberately collaborative practice. And what the learner needs is a more knowledgeable other (MKO) who can share expertise and serve as a model for enacting new skills.

3. **Learning is influenced by context, but may not easily transfer from one context to another.**

   In relation to teachers and TAs: this is a reminder of the importance of setting new learning in a context, and specifying the extent to which it transfers to other contexts. For example, *I do this with the Year 7s but by Year 9 I expect them to...*

4. **Meta-cognition is an important part of the learning process.**

   In relation to teachers and TAs: this is a reminder that, like your teenage students, your TA should be helped to an awareness of her own learning, and also of the ways in which she learns best, and the extent and limits of her knowledge and understanding. This is a reality check for the importance of continuing to learn as a member of the instructional team.

Differentiation

If we ask ourselves why there are now so many TAs working in our schools, the main causal factor is essentially differentiation. The *National Agreement* in 2003/2004 gave teachers in England and Wales the right to Preparation, Planning and Assessment (PPA) time and created the roles of Cover Supervisor and Higher Level Teaching Assistant (HLTA) to ease teachers' workload. The introduction of the Foundation Stage/Phase in England and Wales also increased the numbers of TAs, as learning became more activity based in the early years of schooling. Both of these account for an increase in the numbers of TAs. Even so, differentiation is at the heart of even these initiatives, because they are based on the need to provide a more satisfactory and appropriate education for every child, and that means every individual child – no matter what their individual abilities and needs. This may seem a rather obvious point, but we make it here to remind ourselves that TAs are essentially one of the resources available to teachers when planning for and implementing differentiation.

And so, this section of the book is designed to provide you with:

- a reminder of the diverse needs of learners;
- a basic understanding of what differentiation is;
- an understanding of some ways in which we can differentiate our teaching and students' learning experiences.

Differentiation is the process by which differences between students are accommodated so that all students have the best possible chance of learning. So as teachers, we are required to set suitable learning challenges, respond to students' diverse needs, and overcome potential barriers to learning. This is a tall order, so what does it mean in practical terms?

In 2001 Tim O'Brien and Dennis Guiney proposed a number of 'principles for differentiation' and pointed out that successful differentiation is not about planning to troubleshoot for some students, but must be a practice that is applied to all.
   The principles they proposed were:

1. All children have a right to a high-quality education.
2. Every child can learn.
3. Every teacher can learn.
4. Learning is a process that involves mutual relationships.
5. Progress for all will be expected, recognised and rewarded.
6. People and learning systems can change for the better.

Differentiation is an approach to teaching that attempts to ensure that all students learn well, despite their many differences. Catchphrases which go some way to capturing this concept include: *Coping with differences*, *Learning for all* and *Success for all*. So how do we meet learners' diverse needs? We need to take into account the variety of factors that may affect learning, such as the ability of the students, the different ways in which students learn, and the effectiveness of the teaching approaches we choose to use.

The ability of the students

Some students may have been identified as having Additional Learning Needs or Special Educational Needs (ALN/SEN), but there will be a huge variety of abilities among any class of students. Some may struggle with particular subjects or skills within a subject; others could be 'high flyers' in particular subjects; some will be designated 'more able and talented'.

How people learn

We know that there are a variety of ways in which we may learn best. If you surveyed family or colleagues on how they like to learn or study, you would find a combination of preferences.

- Do they like silence? Or do they prefer some background noise?
- Do they like to create a mind map when thinking through a problem? Or do they find that a list helps them more?

Howard Gardiner's Multiple Intelligences are now commonly known and accepted as valid in education settings, emphasising the variety of ways in which we can measure success. But we should also still consider the earlier identification of learning styles or preferences based on the three modalities of visual, auditory, tactile/kinaesthetic learning.

Learning preferences

Those with *Visual Preferences* (estimated at 60% of students) prefer:

> demonstrations, descriptions, lists, reading by sight; and for noise to be blocked out; they remember faces not names, and are likely to be distracted by movement.

Those with *Auditory Preferences* prefer:

> verbal instructions, listening, dialogues, discussions and plays; they are likely to remember names not faces; they prefer talking through problems and work well in a quiet atmosphere

Those with *Tactile/Kinaesthetic* preferences:

> find it best to take notes when listening or reading, draw or doodle to remember, like hands-on activities, need to be involved and active, learn best when moving; they lose much of what is said, and may have problems sitting and reading.

It is important to note that although children have learning preferences with regards to modalities, research shows that teaching all content in their best modality does *not* equal greater achievement. The *content's* best modality is more important for achievement (Willingham, 2005). For example, as David Sousa points out, if you want students to learn and remember what something looks like, then your presentation should be visual. Orally describing the Roman Coliseum to students is not as effective as showing them a picture or model of it. Likewise, having students read about 1920s Ragtime music would not be as effective as listening to a CD of Scott Joplin playing his famous rags.

Case study: Matthew aged 13

Matthew is in a less able group for French. He is in the middle group for mathematics and in mixed-ability groups for other subjects.

He reports that he finds dictation hard as he cannot record information easily and "the teachers go too quickly". He describes himself as getting in a panic when he has to do creative writing as he cannot sequence his ideas or put them down on paper. He says he does not use big words because he does not know how to spell them. He gets frustrated because "people cannot see my full potential in the use of words".

Matthew is learning to use a computer but it takes him a long time to type and sometimes he cannot read the suggestions given by the software. He says he works three times as hard as others to catch up with coursework. He feels the pressure and goes running to help him relax.

What would you do for Matthew? What would you change about your teaching? You can see that he has been given access to a computer – which is something we often do for students who struggle – but that has not resolved the issue of recording information because he is slow using the keyboard and uncertain of the software. He obviously has some coping skills, as he is aware of his own difficulties, works hard to compensate and runs to reduce stress levels. What more could you do to help Matthew succeed?

The type of teacher we are is determined largely by the way we were taught ourselves – the research suggests this is true despite the intervening years of teacher training/education. Just think: What dangers does this pose for teaching a class of students with a variety of needs? And how on earth can we differentiate to accommodate all students' needs every lesson? Well the simple answer is: we just can't. But there are some things we can do.

Secondary schools begin the process of differentiation by setting or streaming students according to ability. This can be based on general abilities, as well as ability in different core areas such as literacy and numeracy. Interestingly, a review of the use of setting across a school showed:

- no significant differences on overall attainment between setting and mixed ability teaching;
- ability grouping does not contribute much to raising standards of all students;
- lower achieving students show more progress in mixed-ability classes;
- higher achieving students show more progress in set classes.

So some of the possible ways of grouping students (whole school or within class) might include ability, but also:

- a mix of abilities
- gender
- expertise
- friendship.

We can also differentiate in a number of other ways:

- *By task* – different tasks are given to different students to reflect their needs. These can focus upon the same topic/theme or may be entirely different work.
- *By support* – the task may be the same, but different resources can be made available for different learners (e.g. struggling learners could be given definitions for difficult words, scaffolding for writing, or sentence starters for discussions). In terms of human support, more able students could be placed within a group or the TA/teacher might work more closely with a group of struggling students. A way of challenging the more able can be by using advanced written material.
- *By product* – the same task is given, for example, to prepare some writing to persuade an audience, but different learners are asked to present it in different ways; for example, in the style of a poster, pamphlet or magazine article (these require different amounts of text and different relationships between the illustrations and the text). This allows for more demanding features to be introduced for some.
- *By outcome* – students are given the same task with the same resources but have to tackle it in their own way. The outcome shows their ability to complete the task and their understanding of it.

There are advantages and disadvantages to each of these methods, as you'll see in Table 1.1.

Table 1.1 Advantages and disadvantages of different types of differentiation

Differentiation by...	Advantages	Disadvantages
Task	• Work suitable for each student • Failure unlikely, behavioural problems might be reduced • Useful for formative assessment	• Labour intensive for the teacher • May highlight differences • Not useful for summative assessment
Support	• All students produce the same piece of work and feel equal • Failure unlikely, behavioural problems might be reduced • Can be useful for summative assessment	• Labour intensive for the teacher • May highlight differences • Might not be a true reflection of ability
Product	• All students can achieve • Failure unlikely, behavioural problems might be reduced • Can help students work on their weak areas	• Labour intensive • Difficult to provide for a class of 30 • Time consuming • Students might finish at different times
Outcome	• Easy to plan • Useful for summative assessment – clearly shows different levels • Students could work collaboratively	• Without support some students might be restricted • Some students might fail • Difference in abilities could be highlighted • Students could finish at different times

Peter Blatchford and his colleagues from the University of London's Institute of Education reported in 2008 on the large-scale national study of the deployment and impact of TAs (DISS). They found that the amount of individual attention or support students received from the teacher declined when a TA was present, particularly in secondary schools, "showing that the individualization of attention was provided by support staff at the expense of teachers" (p. 12). You can see the logic in this statement; however, it led Blatchford and his fellow researchers to note a conceptual shift: "there are grounds for the conceiving of interactions between support and students as an *alternative* as much as an *additional* form of support" – which was not the intended aim or rationale for the use of TAs.

The challenge that faces schools is to do what we can to meet the diversity of student needs in our classrooms. The remainder of this book will look at ways we can differentiate by support, making effective use of the TAs who are assigned to work with our students.

How things have changed

A long time ago when I was a pupil in my small village primary school, the teacher stood at the front of the classroom and taught the whole class in the same way. Everyone was expected to listen and do the same work; some were able to do a lot of it, others not much. The focus was on content, not on learning and conceptual understanding. There was no discussion over learning styles. If you were not able to keep up, you were left behind. Of course in those days there were no pupils designated as having special or additional needs, because the legislation which extended schooling to all children had not yet been enacted.

Over time teaching changed, as the term *differentiation* entered our vocabulary. Twenty years ago when I first stood in front of the class as a teacher, we had some differentiation, but it usually just consisted of a simpler worksheet! But as time went on, and a better understanding of the extent of the need for differentiation was reached, I began to prepare different tasks for groups in my class and now lesson planning became far more detailed. Differentiation was more about meeting the needs of each individual rather than teaching to include the needs of the whole class.

We know that pupils come to class with different backgrounds, with differences in interests and with differences in how they learn. Good differentiation must take all of this into consideration.

Carol Tomlinson talks about 'responsive' teaching: as teachers we need to respond to differences in students and ensure we meet their needs. We need to be proactive in our differentiation – to be prepared and use the student's IEP (if they have one) to support targets and strategies. We also need to be reactive in our differentiation, differentiating work during the lesson and on the hoof in order to ensure that if the student does not seem to be keeping up, we adapt and re-teach until they do get it!

Here are two contrasting examples of differentiation.

Case study 1: a lesson with poor differentiation

Context – Year 7 Geography Lesson, 27 students of mixed ability

1 Teacher, 1 Teaching Assistant

The teacher knew that there were students in her lesson with differing needs but she did not consult the IEP or her TA to find out exactly what the students could or could not do. But when she delivered a class lesson on the oceans she divided the class into three groups, giving each group a different task.

Group 1 (bright students): find out, using any media, as much information as you can about the different oceans of the world.

Group 2 (average students): find out about the different types of fish present in the oceans of the world.

Group 3 (low ability students): here's a worksheet. Colour the oceans blue and label them!

The teacher had grouped the students according to ability, but was not respectful in the tasks assigned. The third task was not at all challenging and therefore was not respectful to that group of students. We need to ensure that we provide quality in our lessons. The teacher did not use her TA to support the groups as they were all given work she thought they could do without any particular challenge. The TA was just there for crowd control in case the students got bored and resorted to challenging behaviour.

Case study 2: a lesson with good differentiation

Context – Year 9 Biology Lesson, 25 students of mixed ability

1 Teacher, 1 Teaching Assistant

The environment had been prepared before the students entered the class, and the teacher and TA both knew the objective and success criteria of the lesson. The teacher provided the TA with an outline of the lesson and the key aspects and terminology that he wanted her to use when working with the students. The teacher knew the students with IEPs and he had included specific differentiation for them in his planning.

The students entered the classroom and as he had a seating plan they knew where to sit. The student with social communication difficulties was near the interactive white board (IWB) so that he could focus on the lesson. There was no designated chair for the TA so she was able to roam and was available to support any students who needed help.

The lesson began with the teacher setting the scene for the topic of the lesson, using slides to provide the students with the outline and making the lesson meaningful and relevant – worth listening to! Those students with ASD and ADD/ADHD would not be having 'surprises' which may result in challenging behaviour.

The subject was 'The digestive system'. The teacher showed a video clip on the IWB followed by involving the students in dramatising the journey of food through the digestive system! All students were involved. The TA was on hand to support some students who needed instructions repeated and visual prompts were also used to support those students who had auditory recall difficulties.

There was now a need to write up the information! Often this is where challenging behaviour can be seen as those students hitherto involved in the practical aspects of the lesson are now faced with the reality that they have to record the lesson on paper – for some students a seemingly pointless task. The teacher then proceeded to provide the students with a choice of recording options:

*   write an account
*   sequence photographs which were taken by the TA during the lesson
*   use the iPad to sequence and write
*   draw a cartoon strip with sentences/words depending on the ability level
*   dictate the work onto the iPad.

The lesson concluded with the students giving feedback on their work.

You can see from these contrasting accounts of teachers' attempts at differentiation that this is no simple task. It does require additional time and effort. However, we should perhaps consider the advantages and disadvantages of planning for and implementing differentiation strategies during lessons. Successful differentiation means:

- all students are all engaged;
- all students are able to access the lesson material and are therefore learning;
- all students are able to record and review the lesson.

The converse will be true where teachers do not engage with this notion of differentiation: students are less likely to engage with lesson material or activities, they are less likely to learn from the lesson, they will probably be unable to make any meaningful record of the lesson or recall relevant details – all of which is very likely to produce not only dissatisfaction but also disaffection and the associated inappropriate behaviour.

In order for successful differentiation to occur, there needs to be collaboration between all adults in the classroom. Differentiation must not only be in content, but also in our language (see *Top tips* for speech, language and communication), and differentiate our behaviour management (see *Top tips* for SEBD). Differentiation is also a requirement for teachers as shown in the information in the following box.

The *Standards for Registration: Mandatory Requirements for Registration* with the General Teaching Council for Scotland (2012) list, under *Have high expectations of all learners* that "Registered teachers ensure learning tasks are varied, differentiated and devised to build confidence and promote progress of all learners, providing effective support and challenge."

Likewise in England, the *Teachers' Standards: Guidance for School Leaders, School Staff and Governing Bodies* (DfE, 2011) refers to the standard 'Adapt teaching to respond to the strengths and needs of all pupils' and includes the following:

> have a clear understanding of the needs of all pupils, including those with special educational needs; those of high ability; those with English as an additional language; those with disabilities; and be able to use and evaluate distinctive teaching approaches to engage and support them.

Clearly 'distinctive teaching approaches' does not merely refer to handing the student over to a TA.

In conclusion, teachers in differentiated classrooms begin where the students are, not just at the front of a curriculum guide. They accept and build on the understanding that students learn in different ways. They also accept that they must be ready to engage students by appealing to differing interests, and by challenging all students. In differentiated classrooms, teachers provide support for each individual student to learn, understanding that they may learn in different ways and working with the TA to meet the needs of the students. Teachers in differentiated classes use time flexibly and use differing strategies. They use the IEPs as a *tool* to support inclusion and differentiation in order to meet the needs of students in our classrooms. At the Appendix at the end of this chapter you will see an example of a school's provision map (pages 28–9). Many schools are now using this type of approach to provide for the needs of all students, rather than basing provision on IEPs and other individualised plans. You will see that the provision map is organised under the different types of differentiation, so that TAs are only one resource among many at the school's disposal, and that provision is a whole-school approach, rather than the domain of special education or the SENCO.

The Department for Education's *Statistical First Release* on the school workforce in England reported that between spring 2000 and November 2012 the numbers of full-time equivalent teachers in service increased by 36,300 from 405,800 to 442,000. This represents an increase of 8.9%. However, over the most recent years, the teacher numbers have remained relatively flat – at around 440,000. In comparison, the numbers of FTE TAs increased threefold from 79,000 in spring 2000 to 232,300 in November 2012 with the rate of growth slowing in more recent years. However, between November 2011 and 2012 FTE TA numbers increased by 12,500 (5.7%).

- 92% of TAs were female (73% of teachers and 65% of headteachers were female).
- 88% of TAs were white British (the same as teachers).

It may be useful here to remind ourselves of the characteristics of the group we are focusing on. Who are TAs? What are they 'like'? Our research showed us three important features of the TAs who participated in the research.

1. **The majority (84%) were working at Level 2, with only nine (6%) at Level 3, four at Level 4 and none at Level 1.**

    These numbers refer to the levels set by the *National Agreement* and other government guidelines, with the levels representing grades – of pay and expectations – of TAs. Thus at Level 1, the TA would not be expected to have particular formal qualifications, but nor should he or she be allocated particularly expert roles. And so on through Levels 2 and 3, where qualifications and expectations would be higher, through to Level 4, the level expected of those who seek HLTA status, and whose responsibilities can include teaching full classes and supervising other TAs. Decisions about the level at which a TA is employed are made partly at local authority level, sometimes at school level. Why do we even make a point of this particular statistic? You probably will not know the level or grade of the TA who works in your classroom (and it would hardly be appropriate to ask), but we would ask you to consider in a later chapter what distinctions you would make between different levels of work you might assign to the TAs who provide support in your classroom, according to their qualifications and levels of expertise.

2. **Years of experience as a TA ranged from less than one year to 27 years, with an average of 7.7 years (median 7).**

    This statistic is always a good reality check. How much experience does your TA have? How well informed are they about how classrooms work? Have they been in many different schools? Seen many different teachers work? They may actually have spent more time in more classrooms than you have, even though your qualifications will almost always exceed those of your TA. Again, it would be interesting and important to know how experienced your TA is, because they might have quite well-informed opinions about how things could be done differently – if you choose to seek those opinions.

    This demographic relating to years of experience is typical of TAs across the UK. They vary widely in experience and age. In primary schools many TAs begin their work in classrooms as volunteer mums, and then take on a few hours of paid work as it becomes available in the school, and as their own children get older. As volunteers they most often listened to children read or helped out with craft activities, with their responsibilities growing once they are employed – perhaps to work with a student with disabilities or to provide general support in the primary classroom. In secondary schools, this is a less likely scenario, but the initial 'qualifications' for the job have typically been the same for the more experienced TAs: a willingness to 'have a go' and work with even the most difficult of students, despite having little or no training themselves. Training may well have been provided along the way, especially if they support a student with a condition such as autism or dyslexia, but many TAs still receive relatively little training for the work they do.

When a new cohort of TAs enrols on the Foundation Degree course, I always ask them how long they've been working as TAs. This usually ranges from about two or three years (not many of them begin their studies in their first year) to more than 20 years. When you add up all that experience, from a group of about 20 TAs they always have at least 100 years of experience between them! That's not to say that it's all been quality experience, but it does suggest that they've seen what goes on in classrooms, they've usually seen a variety of different teachers and their differing approaches to their work, to their relationships with students, and to how they manage student behaviour. So when it comes to discussing things like teaching methods or behaviour management strategies, they've always got plenty to say, because they have so much experience to draw on.

Jill Morgan

3. **The average number of years of experience working with students with Additional Learning Needs (ALN) was 6.9 years, with a range of less than one year to 25 years.**

This statistic is another reality check, and a reminder of the need to know how experienced and well informed your TA is. Perhaps he or she is a great expert on a particular condition or disability, because of extensive experience supporting a particular student. Or perhaps he or she would really appreciate some basic pointers about how to work in a way which would be most effective.

4. **Some 68% of the TAs stated that they had attended induction training on beginning their employment with the authority; the remainder had not.**

This statistic is likely to vary considerably, depending on where you teach. But again it is a useful reminder that your TA may not even have had a basic introduction to the school or to her role. Has she been given guidelines on general comportment around the school (the issues of professionalism that include dress, use of mobile phones, punctuality, etc.)? You cannot assume that she will know how to behave appropriately in the classroom. Your expectations may also vary from those of other teachers in the school. Likewise she may or may not have received training in effective teaching or behaviour management strategies. Even if she has, her assumptions about what constitutes acceptable behaviour and appropriate responses to student behaviour may not align with your philosophy and preferences. We walk you through some of the process of establishing expectations with your TA in a later chapter.

Results of our research suggested the need to be aware of the following:

- TAs may or may not have had induction training on first being employed; therefore may or may not have had an overview of the basic elements of professionalism (punctuality, dress, etc); even so, your expectations of their conduct in the classroom may need to be clarified.
- Your TA's experience of working in classrooms may be very little or very extensive – and anything in between – in either case the TA may have valuable opinions to offer.
- Your TA's experience of working with students with ALN may also be extensive or very limited; your TA may therefore be looking for considerable guidance from you, or may be comfortable with her assigned role and be able to offer you some guidance on how to best work with her assigned student.

Working with teens

And lastly, a note on working with teenagers. The teen years are a time of change and development, and teachers have long recognised that adolescents have particular characteristics that make them a unique and sometimes challenging group to teach. Much of this has been attributed to hormonal changes in the teen body, but the most recent research into the adolescent brain, using MRI (magnetic resonance imaging) techniques, is suggesting some alternative explanations for teenage behaviour.

The teenage brain has been considered to be more like an adult brain than the brain of a child. However, it now appears that the brain continues to develop well into adulthood, only being fully established by about age 25 to 30, so the teenage brain is continuing to undergo significant development. As a child learns and gains new experiences, synapses are developed in the brain, but the brain is so sophisticated that it regularly goes through a process of pruning these synapses, retaining only those which are most often used, to create greater efficiency. In addition, as areas of the brain mature, the pathways in the brain along which impulses or messages pass become coated in myelin. Much like the insulation on electrical wires which keeps the current contained and focused, the myelin also improves the efficiency of the brain. The last area of the brain to become established in this way would appear to be the frontal lobes, which deal with areas such as:

- planning
- organisation
- self-control and impulse inhibition
- multi-tasking
- empathy
- judgement
- adapting to change.

Small wonder that these are the very characteristics that seem to be lacking in teenagers. They are not deliberately trying to make our lives difficult – their brains are not yet fully wired for the levels of maturity we expect of them in these areas. In addition, the amygdala which controls emotional response matures much more quickly than the frontal lobes, so decisions during the teen years are more likely to be made based on emotion and impulse than on rational thought or carefully considered judgement. Appendix 3.7 provides a *Top tips* page on working with teens, which you might like to share with your TA.

Chapter summary

In this chapter we have considered two important elements of the teacher's role: working with and directing the work of Teaching Assistants, and differentiating work so that all students can access the curriculum. These elements are clearly specified in the published standards for teachers across the UK, and now form part of the expectations of school inspectorates. Because of the importance of differentiation, we have provided an overview as a reminder of the variety of ways in which that can be approached. The employment of TAs in such large numbers has been based on differentiation by support, and so we have also provided an overview of the statistics relating to TAs, and have highlighted the need for providing training to TAs so that they can be effective in their support role. This is not simply a book about including the TA in the team (although that is important, as we discuss in a later chapter); we see a clear need for schools to confirm TAs' skill levels and take deliberate steps to enhance those skills so that the TA's contribution to the classroom team is maximised. And lastly, we took a brief look at some of the most recent research on the teenage brain – as a reminder of the challenges of working with this particular age group.

Bibliography

Blatchford, P., Bassett, P., Brown, P., Martin, C., Russell, A. and Webster, R. with Babayigit, S. and Haywood, N. (2008) *Deployment and Impact of Support Staff in Schools and the Impact of the National Agreement Results from Strand 2 Wave 1 – 2005/06.* London: DCSF.

Cowley, S. (2013) *The Seven T's of Practical Differentiation (Alphabet Sevens).* CreateSpace Independent Publishing.

DCELLS (2009) *Becoming a Qualified Teacher: Handbook of Guidance.* Guidance Circular No: 017/2009. Cardiff: WAG.

Department for Education (2011) *Teacher Standards. Guidance for School Leaders, School Staff and Governing Bodies.* London: DfE.

Department for Education (2013) *Statistical First Release: School Workforce in England, November 2012.* London: DfE. Available at: www.education.go v.uk/researchandstatistics/statistics/a00223460/ school-workforceengland-nov-2012 (accessed: 20.4.15).

Department for Education (2015) *Special Educational Needs and Disability Code of Practice: 0 to 25 years.* London: Department for Education.

Education and Training Inspectorate (N. Ireland) (2006) *Effective Use of Assistants for pupils with Special Educational Needs in Mainstream Schools.* Report of an Inspection survey, 2005–6. Belfast: ETI (NI)

Estyn (2010) *Guidance for the Inspection of Secondary Schools.* Cardiff: Estyn.

General Teaching Council for Northern Ireland (2011) *Teaching: The Reflective Profession*, 3rd edition. Belfast: GTCNI. Available at: www.gtcni.org.uk/index.cfm/area/information/page/ProfStandard (accessed: 20.4.15).

General Teaching Council for Scotland (2012) *The Standards for Registration: Mandatory Requirements for Registration with the General Teaching Council for Scotland.* Edinburgh: GTCS. Available at: http://www.gtcs.org.uk/standards (accessed: 20.4.15).

Gershon (2013) *How to use Differentiation in the Classroom: The Complete Guide: 3.* CreateSpace Independent Publishing.

HMIe (2007) *How Good is Our School? The Journey to Excellence: Part 3.* Edinburgh: HM Inspectorate of Education.

Martin-Denham, S. (2015) *Teaching Children and Young People with Special Educational Needs and Disabilities.* London: Sage.

Morgan, J. and Ashbaker, B.Y. (2009) *Supporting and Supervising your Teaching Assistant.* London: Continuum.

Morgan, J. and Ashbaker, B.Y. (2012) Teachers supervising teaching assistants: Assigned role or discretionary behaviour? Reflections from the United Kingdom. In Ibrahim Duyar and Anthony H. Normore (eds)

Discretionary Behavior and Performance in Educational Organizations: The Missing Link in Educational Leadership and Management (Advances in Educational Administration, Volume 13). Bingley: Emerald Group Publishing Limited, pp. 249–74.

O'Brien, T. and Guiney, D. (2001) *Differentiation in Teaching and Learning: Principles and Practices.* Abingdon: Continuum.

Parker, M., Lee, C., Gunn, S., Heardman, K., Knight, R.H., Pittman, M. and Richards, G. and Armstrong, F. (2007) *Key Issues for Teaching Assistants: Working in Diverse and Inclusive Classrooms.* London: Routledge.

Willingham, G.T. (2005) *Do Visual, Auditory, and Kinesthetic Learners Need Visual, Auditory, and Kinesthetic Instruction?* Available at: www.aft.org/ae/summer2005/willingham (accessed 17.7.15).

Wolfe, P. (2011) *The Adolescent Brain: A Work in Progress.* Mind Matters, Inc. Available at: http://patwolfe.com/2011/09/the-adolescent-brain-a-work-in-progress (accessed: 20.4.15).

Chapter 1 Appendix: exemplar of a school provision map

General differentiation	More Able and Talented (MAT)	Additional Learning Needs (ALN)
Differentiation of resources		
• White board activities • Starter tasks to model learning and practice tasks • Powerpoint presentation /games • Visual resources	• Extension games – web based on occasion	• Resources to aid learning • Visual resources, text and concrete objects to aid learning
Differentiation by task		
• Model for the task • Shared group ideas/paired work • Classroom differentiation • Group roles/differentiated groups and partners • Assessment for learning • KWL grids • Thinking time/talking time • Lollipop sticks – no hands up • Talking partners • Using whiteboards • Peer support – students support each other with ideas, contributions valued by all • Buddying used for seating • Paired or partner work – scribe ideas • Time allocated for task • KWL grid at beginning of topic – plan to reflect students' interest and understanding • Differentiated questions • Language used to individuals • Questioning • Use of questioning, giving thinking time/response partners/scaffolding questioning • Planning for different learning styles using visual auditory and kinaesthetic tasks to appeal to different children	• Differentiated models for the task • Extension tasks • Challenge tasks • Individual targeting of children in lessons • Text more challenging • Independent practical activities, individual learning • Projects • Degree of thinking needed • Degree of problem solving required • Open-ended tasks • Time allocated for task • Extension work • Independent research time and presentation of work • Expect able students to articulate what has been learnt • Give an oral commentary with the more able in mind • Use of questioning • Increase pace and less explanation of tasks to encourage independent learning and thinking	• Familiarity of tasks • Motivation, attitude, attention span and effort • Concepts involved • Prior knowledge, skill, expertise or interest • Learning preferences • Increased visual aids/ modelling • Set achievable tasks of children involved • Time allocated for specific tasks • Targeted tasks to interest the students • Model language needed for the tasks • Prepare questions targeted on particular students that reflect their needs an personalities

© 2016, *Achieving Outstanding Classroom Support in Your Secondary School*, J. Morgan, C. Jones and S. Booth-Coates, Routledge

Differentiation by support		
• Targeted teacher time • Varied group membership • Support for reading • Small group support • Spelling groups • Individual targeting of children in lessons • Classroom differentiation	• Identify able students' shared needs and group accordingly • Peer support and targeted teacher time • Give able students roles in group work that reflect their abilities • Have group / student targets, not just class targets • Set targets with high expectations of tasks with more able students • Use peer editing or marking • Encourage use of deciding or following SC (success criteria) to succeed	• TA support or class teacher support • Use of TA to assess capabilities for the task • One-to-one discussion with TA expectation of tasks • TA support – questioning and understanding of tasks
Differentiation by response/outcome		
• Shared clear tasks and learning outcomes • Learning objectives and success criteria in every lesson • Make time for individual feedback • Support children while working • Targeted marking feedback • Oral feedback • Scaffold and model the task • Paired work • Scribe/group roles • Differentiated outcome • Model text and presentation of tasks	• Decide on own success criteria – improve own targets • Promote self-evaluation • Help able students to contribute to the success of others • Ask abler students to articulate the skills involved in completing particular tasks • Decide together on the objectives to be addressed by able students – styles of response and criteria for evaluation • Leading the learning – methods used in the presentation of their ideas • Involve students in modelling (if appropriate) • Ask able students to articulate explanations and principles • Model only those which able students need to know	• Success criteria condensed into more manageable targets • Oral support given during the task • Illustrated dictionaries – word banks • Use of writing frames • Access to word processing

© 2016, *Achieving Outstanding Classroom Support in Your Secondary School*, J. Morgan, C. Jones and S. Booth-Coates, Routledge

Chapter 2

What the research tells us about TAs

In 2003 the UK government published the document *Raising Standards and Tackling Workload: A National Agreement* as a move towards reducing teacher workload and raising standards in schools in England and Wales. Agreed between government, employers and school workforce unions, the subsequent changes in teachers' contractual obligations allocated teachers a half day per week of PPA time (Preparation, Planning and Assessment) from September 2005, and excused them from being 'routinely required' to perform the clerical and administrative tasks listed in the nearby box. These tasks do not require a teacher's professional judgement and could therefore be taken on by someone without a teaching qualification. So this same legislation had quite a significant effect on TAs as well as teachers:

- Although many TAs had already been assigned some of the 25 roles listed in the box, more of them passed over to TAs as teachers could be excused from them.
- It introduced HLTA (Higher Level Teaching Assistant) status. TAs can gain HLTA status by putting together a portfolio of reflective accounts of how their current work and past experience meet the standards for HLTA status as set out by the legislation. No training is involved, except in relation to compiling the portfolio and other paperwork. HLTA is not a qualification, and this status has waned in popularity in parts of England, but continues strong in Wales. TAs who are employed in this capacity would normally be considered a Level 4 (on a scale of 1 to 4) for remuneration purposes and would be expected to have some formal qualifications such as NVQ (National Vocational Qualification) or BTEC.
- It introduced a potential new role for TAs: that of Cover Supervisor, or what is essentially in-house supply cover. This was especially important given the allocation of PPA time to all teachers, equivalent to 10% of the school week. In order to take on the role of Cover Supervisor, ideally TAs should have HLTA status, as they can be asked to plan and teach lessons, as well as supervising other TAs who may be assigned to the classes they cover. If the Cover Supervisor has expertise in a particular area (e.g. sport or music), schools can choose to have them teach that subject rather than covering the curriculum area of the teacher whose PPA time they are covering.

The *National Agreement* brought TAs into the limelight and recognised their potential for easing teachers' workload. This was one of the aims of the agreement, the ultimate aim being to raise standards in schools across England and Wales.

The *National Agreement* was certainly not the first acknowledgement of the contribution that support staff make to the education system – in the UK or elsewhere in the world. Since the 1990s there has been a growing body of research into TAs' work – based initially on their changing roles and responsibilities, then inevitably on the efficacy of their work in those roles, and moving on to the need for systematic supervision for them. (You can find items relating to this research, including a literature review from 2007, in the Bibliography at the end of this chapter, and in Appendix 1 at

Administrative and clerical tasks teachers should not routinely be required to undertake under the *National Agreement* of 2003.

- Collecting money
- Chasing absences
- Bulk photocopying
- Copy typing
- Producing standard letters – teachers may be required to contribute in formulating the content of standard letters
- Producing class lists
- Record keeping and filing – teachers may be required to contribute to the content of records

- Classroom display
- Analysing attendance figures
- Processing exam results
- Collating pupil reports
- Administering work experience
- Administering examinations
- Invigilating examinations
- Administering teacher cover
- ICT trouble shooting and minor repairs

- Commissioning new ICT equipment
- Ordering supplies and equipment
- Stocktaking
- Cataloguing, preparing, issuing and maintaining equipment and materials
- Minuting meetings
- Coordinating and submitting bids
- Seeking and giving personnel advice
- Managing pupil data
- Inputting pupil data

Many of these tasks may require teacher input (e.g. setting exam questions) or teacher action (e.g. making use of the data for reports or instructional decisions).

the back of the book). Since the turn of the century, some of this interest in the work of TAs was prompted by legislation, such as the No Child Left Behind Act (2004) in the United States, which stipulated that TAs (paraprofessionals) working in Title I programmes were required to have two years of college and work 'under the direction' of a professional educator. Although Title I is specific to disadvantaged groups (similar to the UK's Head Start and Early Start programmes), it is the second largest employer of TAs in the US education system. So this had a significant impact, both in terms of raising awareness of what TAs actually do and in terms of an increase in the number of college courses for TAs. These were largely Associate Degree programmes (similar to the Foundation degree in the UK) but there was no requirement for TAs to have studied in an area that directly related to education.

The largest employer of TAs in the United States has, like the UK, always been special education, and the re-authorisation of the Individuals with Disabilities Education Act (IDEA) of 1997 stipulated for the first time that TAs could be used to provide services to students with disabilities, on condition that they were 'appropriately trained and supervised'. TAs had been providing such services for decades before these NCLB or IDEA were enacted, and neither Act defined what supervision or direction should look like. With no definition, and therefore no accountability, the legislation lacked teeth and has largely been unenforceable, except in a few instances where parents of children with disabilities have taken the local school district (education authority) to tribunal, challenging the provision made for their child. These cases will sometimes include reference to a poorly qualified or unsupervised TA being the main support for the child.

The requirement for supervision of the work of TAs in the UK has received even less attention, despite the stipulation in the *National Agreement* that there be "a proper system of direction and supervision for them". Indeed it still receives little attention in teacher training programmes, despite featuring in the standards for teachers, as noted in the previous chapter. A 2010 report on the implementation of the *National Agreement* in Wales expressed concern over appropriate deployment of TAs and the need for TAs to receive training commensurate with their roles. It also highlighted the need:

to ensure that teachers, particularly new entrants, were trained about how to work with support staff to best effect. There was also a need to enable support staff and teachers to plan together and for classroom-based support staff to be given their own planning and preparation time where appropriate.

After commenting on the need for an increase in the numbers of TAs in order to implement the conditions of the *National Agreement*, the DfES publication *Time for Standards* stated that "Teaching assistants who interact with pupils in relation to teaching and learning, must do so within a regulated system of supervision and leadership operated by the pupils' classroom/subject teacher" (DfES, 2002, p. 11).

The DISS research

Subsequent to the *National Agreement*, the education departments of England and Wales jointly funded the *Deployment and Impact of Support Staff (DISS)* project – a large-scale, five-year piece of research (2003–8) investigating how TAs in England and Wales were being used and how their work impacted on students and staff. The DISS project investigated practice in primary, secondary and special schools, and included surveys and observations of teachers and support staff, with well over 5,000 students also involved.

Main findings of the DISS research (2003–8)

- TAs now have a predominantly instructional role, supporting lower-attaining pupils and those with SEN.
- Teachers have welcomed the easing of their workload through wider use of TAs and the allocation of PPA time.
- In essence many TAs have become the primary 'teachers' for this group of pupils.
- This arrangement works well for teachers, because it allows them to teach the rest of the class, knowing that the pupils with additional learning needs are getting individual attention.
- Logically, however, the more support pupils get from TAs (who may not have formal qualifications), the less they get from teachers (who must have formal qualifications), and
- The support these pupils are receiving is really an alternative form of provision rather than additional support.
- TA-to-pupil interactions were found to be less effective (less educationally valuable) than teacher-to-pupil interactions.
- Pupils with the highest levels of SEN are most likely to experience negative effects of TA support, as their academic progress appears to be far slower than pupils with SEN who receive no support from TAs. This is true even when other factors (such as socio-economic status, age, etc.) are taken into account.

(See Blatchford et al., 2009)

You will find some links to online information about the findings of DISS in the Bibliography, and a brief summary of the main findings in the nearby box. As you will see from the information in the box, many of the conclusions from the research are positive – reduced workload (as intended) for teachers, support for students with additional learning needs, support for appropriate student behaviour. June Stewart's 2009 small-scale study of the impact of Classroom Assistants (CAs) in

Scotland showed similar results to the DISS findings: CAs helped teachers focus on teaching by undertaking a range of non-teaching tasks; they provided more adult attention for students; and they helped to manage behaviour. The CAs themselves highlighted the need for "consultation, planning and collaboration" with their teachers. However, some of the evidence from the DISS research looked pretty damning – particularly the conclusion that pupils who get the most support from TAs may make less progress than similar pupils who receive no additional support. The authors of the research were keen to point out that TAs have little or no control over the ways in which they are deployed and should not therefore be blamed for the lack of progress:

> this situation is not the fault of TAs. Instead, it is attributable to decisions made – often with the best of intentions – about them, *together with inadequate training for teachers on how to work with TAs, and a lack of opportunities for them to properly brief TAs before lessons.*
>
> *(Blatchford et al., 2009; emphasis added)*

Subsequent to the DISS research, a series of research projects relating to the work of TAs (although largely confined to schools in England) have presented findings, with increasing levels of detail. These have included the Making a Statement (MaSt) research into the experiences of students with statements of SEN in relation to TAs, and the Effective Deployment of TAs (EDTA), both headed by researchers at the Institute of Education in London. The 2013 final report for the MaSt project detailed the findings, which were based on interviews with teachers, SENCOs and TAs, as well as week-long shadowing of the 48 Year 5 pupils who had participated, and who either had moderate learning difficulties or SEBD. The authors of the report were complimentary about the diligence with which schools approached the provision for these pupils in what could only be considered difficult financial times. However, five major concerns emerged from the data, which can be found in the nearby box.

Five concerns identified by the Making a Statement (MaSt) study into the experiences of pupils with statements for SEN

1. *The high degree of separation and TA support that characterised the school experiences of the pupils with SEN.* Compared with their peers these pupils spent far more time away from mainstream settings (and therefore the teacher and their peers) and were almost constantly accompanied by a TA, as their learning occurred far more often in one-to-one sessions with the TA rather than with the rest of the class.
2. *TAs had more responsibility for the pupils with statements than the teachers.* This included both planning and teaching. Some TAs had developed alternative schemes of work and interventions, and were the main instructional decision-maker for the pupils. This led to the third concern.
3. *An overall lower quality of teaching input,* reducing the likelihood of closing the attainment gap for these pupils.
4. *The gaps in knowledge of how to best meet the needs of pupils with SEN – for both teachers and TAs.* Although this was a primary school setting, teachers did not feel fully prepared by their initial training. They relied on the TAs who – although they were no more knowledgeable than the teachers – at least had considerable knowledge about the individual pupils.
5. *The lack of a cohesive approach to meeting the needs of pupils with SEN,* with schools largely relying on providing the specified number of hours of TA support.

Referring to TAs as a 'valuable resource', Rob Webster and Peter Blatchford who led the research concluded that the MaSt study "provides further evidence that schools need to fundamentally re-think the common approaches to the ways TAs are deployed and prepared. School leaders and teachers need to think more inclusively about pupils with SEN and ensure their learning needs are not met principally by TAs" (Webster and Blatchford, 2013, p. 3).

These conclusions were supported by further research, also from London's Institute of Education (see Radford et al., 2015) which provided greater detail of the interactions between TAs and pupils. This is where TAs most directly influence students and student learning. Given the high proportion of students with additional learning and support needs who work one-to-one with a TA, or whose work is closely supervised by a TA, these interactions are key. Four features of TA-student interactions were noted. TAs tended to:

1. Close down talk, asking closed, rather than open questions, and supplying the answers rather than leading students through the process of working out the answers for themselves.
2. Emphasise task completion (what the student has done) rather than focusing on learning and understanding (what he has learned).
3. 'Stereo' teach, basically repeating what the teacher has said, perhaps slightly re-phrased to facilitate understanding, perhaps repeated verbatim as a reminder to students who find it hard to concentrate or follow instructions.
4. Provide inaccurate or vague explanations to students, whether this be teacher instructions, processes to be followed or concepts taught.

Michael Giangreco, a researcher at the University of Vermont, has been studying the deployment of TAs (paraprofessionals in the United States) for many years. He and colleague Stephen Broer concluded in 2005 that "paraprofessionals have served as an analgesic for the perceived pressures of including more diverse populations of students with disabilities. Unfortunately, to date we have no compelling evidence that this model is an effective educational support for students with disabilities" (Giangreco and Broer, 2005, p. 24). Ten years later, the UK research we have cited here has essentially furnished compelling evidence that the model is *not* an effective one.

With colleagues Mary Beth Doyle and Jesse Suter, Giangreco (Giangreco et al., 2012) has also concluded that reliance on TAs/paraprofessionals can be totally acceptable, but only if four important conditions are present:

1. Roles are appropriate (e.g. supplemental teacher-planned instruction, facilitating student-to-student interactions, or taking on non-instructional roles so that teachers can engage more often with students with SEN /ALN).
2. Training for TAs is adequate to their roles, and ongoing.
3. TAs are not asked to undertake inappropriate roles (e.g. being the main provider of instruction, liaising with families, making instructional decisions, or adapting curriculum) which require a teacher's professional judgement.
4. TAs are adequately supervised on an ongoing basis.

There is a body of research which shows that TAs can be very effective in their work when they are assigned to deliver very structured programmes or interventions. This should not come as a surprise. But these issues raised by Giangreco and his colleagues will be discussed in the remaining chapters of this book: how to deploy TAs effectively in your classroom; how to enhance their effectiveness; how you can work together with TAs within the constraints of the secondary school system. We seek to address the lack of training that is typical for teachers in how to best work with TAs by presenting practical ways for you to tackle these issues.

Research in Wales

As we noted in the Introduction, we conducted our own research into best practice for TAs working in secondary schools in a Welsh Local Authority. We surveyed TAs across the authority for their views, supplemented by a focus group discussion with a small group of TAs. But we also conducted focus groups with students in one of the local secondary schools to gain a perspective from the point of view of the consumer, as it were. Here is a summary of what we found out from the students, and then from the TAs.

What the students had to say

We started our series of focus groups with the School Council, representing Years 8–11. When we asked them: *What do you think TAs do? What's their job?* They seemed to have a good grasp of why TAs are in our classrooms:

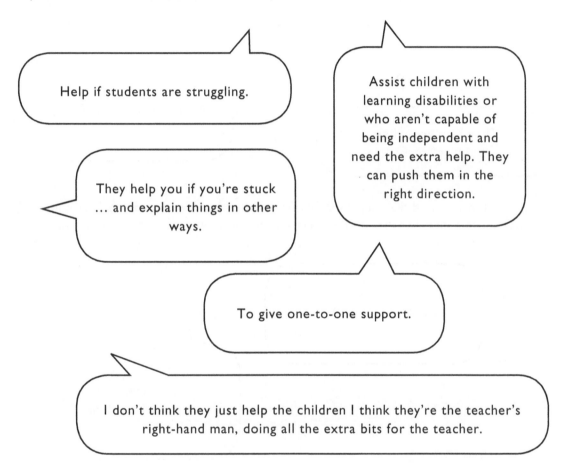

All of that seems quite accurate, and when we put the same questions to a group of pupils in the same school who spend all their time in the specialist teaching facility receiving support from TAs, their answers were similar. They also highlighted the pastoral role which many TAs take on, and the fact that TAs support teachers as well as students:

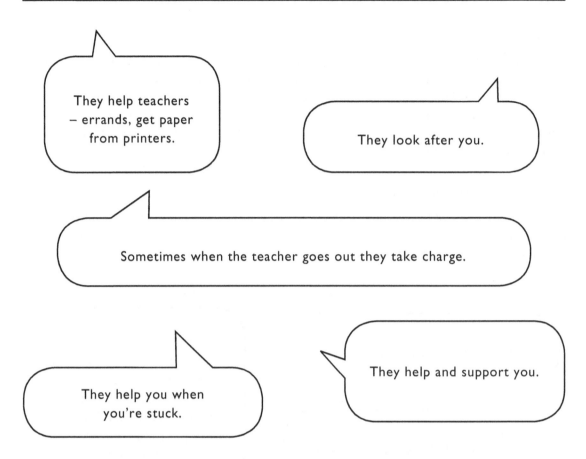

However, when we asked the same question of a group of pupils with additional learning needs who were supported by TAs in mainstream classrooms, the answers were a little different:

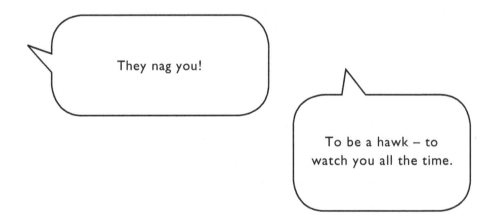

This is obviously not such a positive view, but it is a useful one, because this book is primarily about the situations that these students have experienced – the classroom where the student with some sort of learning or behavioural difficulty attends mainstream classes supported by a TA. And that means your classroom if you are a mainstream, curriculum subject teacher; and your joint responsibility with the SENCO or other member of staff who oversees the work of TAs. So the students' comments here highlight some of the issues relating to TA support, which we will be addressing in the later chapters.

We then asked each of the groups of students how they thought TAs were generally viewed by students. The school council gave these opinions:

- Not respected, for example if a TA told a student off, they would be like 'You can't tell me off, you're not a teacher.'
- In primary the TAs are more highly looked upon than secondary, the kids in secondary think they're better than the TAs.
- People don't take them that seriously.

And they had an idea why this might be the case:

- In primary a TA sticks with one class, in secondary they go around different classes with a student so people don't have that much respect for them.

This again brings us to that situation of the itinerant TA, who follows a particular student from class to class, giving support as needed. Essentially these students saw this as having a negative effect on the TA's credibility.

We also asked the School Council: *What's the relationship between the TAs and the teachers?*

- There's one in my maths class and they usual converse, to check opinions.
- In primary they are quite strong; in secondary the teachers hardly talk to each other.
- In my [subject] class they talk a lot and do seem to have a good relationship.

They have obviously experienced a mix among the teacher–TA teams they have seen, but again they showed their perception by adding:

- In primary the TA is with one teacher, but in secondary they are moving around so they can't build a relationship.

They recognised that being an itinerant TA makes it difficult to develop a working relationship with the teacher – or rather, with the many teachers they may encounter every day. And likewise the difficulty for the teacher who sees a stream of TAs coming through her class each day with each change of lesson, and who therefore can find it difficult to build relationships with each one of them.

Best and worst of having TA support

We also asked the students who received support in mainstream classes:

1. What's the best thing about having a TA helping you with your work?
2. What's the worst thing about having a TA helping you with your work?

We have already suggested in the Introduction that you ask yourself this type of question:

1. What do you think are the advantages – for you, as a teacher – of having TA support in your classroom?
2. What are the disadvantages – for you as a teacher – of having TA support in your classroom?

From the point of view of the students, the best thing appeared to be:

• They help you when you need help.

Which sounds like the perfect answer, and is surely what you would want a TA to do. But they also said:

• They can answer all the questions.
• They give you the answers.

That may be the 'best' thing from some of the students' point of view – having someone do your work and thinking for you – but it is not likely to be what teachers want TAs to do. So that is another issue that we will need to address in a later chapter.

Asked what they thought was the worst thing about having a TA, they said:

• They're annoying because they keep nagging you and don't leave you alone.
• They don't let you sit next to your friends.
• The older ones nag you more – they don't understand you.
• They sit next to you all the time, like a shadow.
• Even when you don't need help they're still there helping you.
• They treat us like we're in Nursery, but we're in Comp now.
• They help you more when you don't need it and then when you need the help it's like they've gone deaf.
• They're like another mother with you.

The students certainly had a lot to say in response to this question, and we saw two main categories of response emerging:

• Student independence
• Appropriateness of support.

These are related, of course, because the type of support TAs provide to individual students needs to be appropriate, in the sense that it should only be as much as the student needs, and not so much that it encourages dependence. But it also needs to be appropriate in that it should be based on a working relationship which challenges and encourages students, facilitating learning and promoting self-esteem. This is not always easy to accomplish, and teenagers can be very sensitive, so this aspect of the TA's work – how they relate to the students and how they treat them – is not a minor consideration.

The picture that emerges

Are you seeing the themes that are emerging here from the responses the students have given? These are some themes we identified:

1. **It is difficult for teachers to develop working relationships with TAs who move around with assigned pupils.**

    This is a first and very important theme, and really provides the impetus for this book. Even the students were able to identify this issue, and we acknowledge that it is not easy for secondary school teachers to develop solid working relationships with TAs – the sort of relationships that allow for effective use of TAs to support learning for the students you are jointly assigned to teach when those TAs are assigned to individual students. Or at least, it is not a simple matter. We are certainly not saying that it is impossible, and that is some of what the remaining chapters of the book will clarify. We know from the research on co-teaching that relationships among staff make a difference – that staff who have a positive working relationship, governed by mutual respect, will work more effectively and pleasantly together. As 'ships that pass in the night' it is obviously much more difficult for you to develop this type of relationship.

2.   TAs may not be accorded the same level of respect as teachers.

It is commonly said that respect has to be earned, and some TAs may not behave in ways which command respect, but in our research this was not evident from the students' responses. They seemed to be aware of a general lack of respect, rather than attributing it to anything the TAs themselves had said or done. You know that as a teacher you have to establish your own authority and earn the respect of your students. But it is not quite that simple for TAs, who may lack the confidence to assert their own authority, who may feel that they are not treated as someone with authority in the school, and who can easily be seen as babysitters for the 'bad boys'. In a later chapter we will be looking at ways in which TAs' credibility can be enhanced, because a TA who is not respected will not be able to be effective in her work. Students need to know that she is a person of authority who teachers trust to provide the support they need.

3.   The way some TAs approach their work suggests that they have insufficient understanding of what constitutes best practice in supporting students in their work, and promoting student independence.

Some TAs support students with very particular needs, and you may well feel that they are the experts and should be responsible for providing the support those students need. This is a healthy and helpful attitude in many ways, because it suggests that you will be willing to look to the TA for information and suggestions. But there are also some basic principles of good practice, in relation to teaching and behaviour, which are necessary for every student – principles which the TA may not ever have been taught. If a TA has attended very little training (and induction training is not a requirement across the whole of the UK, let alone further training in providing effective support), then she cannot be expected to have a broad repertoire of effective strategies to use. She may also have experienced examples of poor practice in some of the classrooms where she works. Hopefully these will be the minority, and she will also have good practice examples to compare with and follow. But osmosis, as you know, is not really the best method of learning or gaining skills. So in this respect your expertise is likely to be greater than hers, and can be shared, for the benefit of the students you have joint responsibility for. As we have seen from the research on TA–student interactions, it would seem that many TAs do not have sufficient expertise in supporting and enhancing learning for the students who need it most.

What the TAs had to say for themselves

We also asked TAs to rate a series of statements, from *Strongly agree* to *Strongly disagree,* based around the following five themes:

- Expectations of the TA.
- Feeling valued.

- Working with the teacher.
- Professional development.
- Support received.

Here are the highlights of what they told us.

Expectations

- Eight out of ten told us that they were *aware of what was expected of them*. A similar 75% *agreed/strongly agreed* with the statement: *I have knowledge of the children's IEPs/ Targets*.
- However less than half *agreed* with *I feel that the school is aware of my strengths and skills*, and a similar proportion a*greed* with *I feel the school uses my strengths and skills well*.
- Seven out of ten felt that they were *encouraged to use their initiative within their own area/ child*, and six out of ten stated that they *keep a record of the work carried out*.

Feeling valued

Three statements related to whether the TAs feel valued.

- Almost eight out of ten *agreed* with: *My opinion is valued by teachers with regards to individual pupils*.
- Similarly six out of ten a*greed* with *I feel I am a valued partner with regards to the child's learning in the classroom*.
- Four out of ten *agreed* with *I feel valued in all areas of school life*.

Positive extended comments in relation to this question related to *being thanked or appreciated* by most teachers (although many respondents commented that appreciation varied among staff members, and generally did not include senior management). Less positive comments included:

- not being included in all aspects of school life;
- staff not explaining expectations or sharing information;
- TAs' skills being under-utilised.

Eight out of ten *agreed/strongly agreed* with *I feel my work in school impacts on the children's learning*. Open-ended responses relating to this statement included:

- providing differentiation;
- supporting children both academically and emotionally.

Working with the teacher

Two statements related to working with the teacher. In response to the first – *I have allocated time to plan within the school timetable* – less than three out of ten rated this as *agree/strongly agree*. For the second – *I plan and evaluate with the teacher* – only two out of ten *agreed*. Open-ended comments consistently showed why:

- No time allocated for planning and/or evaluating with the teacher.

Professional development

In relation to professional development opportunities, more than six out of ten *agreed* that they were *invited to attend 'In School Training Sessions,'* 50% that they were *encouraged to attend further off-site training*, and seven out of ten with *I would like to update my skills regularly by attending refresher courses*. However, only four out of ten *agreed* with *I am encouraged to share my training with other staff*.

Support received

There was a very positive response (80%) to the statement *I know who to approach if I have a problem*. Likewise 70% stated that they *receive a good level of support from the SENCO*, and 55% *agreed* that they *receive a good level of support from the classroom teachers*.

One of the open-ended questions we asked related to areas of difficulty: *Which areas of your work do you find difficult? Why are these difficult?* Almost 50% of the TAs referred to lack of continuity from one lesson to the next when working with different students or because of timetabling issues. But other comments also related to:

- Working with staff who do not use TAs effectively (including issues of differentiation).
- Having to provide support in subject areas in which they have no confidence.
- Lack of respect from students.

Positive views

We also asked TAs about the positive aspects of their work: *Which areas of your job do you feel you do particularly well?* and *What in your opinion has enabled this success?* Almost half of the TAs referred to the positive relationships with students or a positive atmosphere at work. Other aspects included the satisfaction of seeing students succeed, and knowing what the teacher expected of them in a lesson.

These are some of the same themes recurring from the focus groups with students, which not surprisingly align with the findings of the national studies, suggesting that the issues are pervasive. The questions in the self-audit we provided in the Introduction derive from these questions posed to the TAs, so hopefully you will have already taken the opportunity to consider some of these issues from a teacher or SENCO's perspective.

Teachers and TAs collaborating

There is a much smaller body of professional or academic research relating to teachers and TAs working together. Although a great deal has been written about co-teaching, the dynamics of two teachers sharing a classroom are obviously quite different from teacher and TA working together. Dr Cristina Devecchi, as part of her PhD research, investigated teachers and TAs working together in a secondary school in Cambridgeshire (you can find further details in the Bibliography). From analysis of her data, she came to see this collaboration as consisting of three types of sharing: sharing knowledge, sharing physical space and sharing agency.

Sharing knowledge. This included specialist or technical knowledge about teaching strategies and resources (including lesson planning), knowledge of individual students (for which teachers were often dependent on the TAs), and knowledge about each other (their professional needs and expectations, but also sharing personal details and concerns).

Reflective questions: three types of sharing – knowledge, space and agency

Sharing knowledge

- When and how will you share your specialist or technical knowledge about teaching strategies and resources (including lesson planning) with your TA?

- When and how will you have your TA share her knowledge of individual students with you?

- When and how will you and your TA share knowledge about each other (your professional needs and expectations, as well as personal details and concerns)?

Sharing space

- Are you comfortable having your TA move freely around the classroom?

- Do you feel you can trust her to give more general support rather than remaining with an assigned student?

- When and how will you communicate your preferences to her?

Sharing agency

- How much independence are you prepared to allow your TA?

- To what extent would you have her take initiative?

- What types of decision do you feel you can trust her with?

- How much authority are you willing to share with her?

- How will you convey this to her? And to your students?

© 2016, *Achieving Outstanding Classroom Support in Your Secondary School*, J. Morgan, C. Jones and S. Booth-Coates, Routledge

Sharing space. Cristina Devecchi warns against taking too simplistic a view of this as simply sharing the physical space of the classroom. She also sees it as including the freedom to move freely around in the classroom, including for TAs who were assigned to support a specific student. In her research, teachers and TAs explained that this sharing was significant because "this is the place where [teachers] are in charge and where they set the rules, the expectations, where they can control their practice ... For TAs entering this space can be stressful, sharing it can be a reward" (Devecchi, 2005, p. 3). So this sharing of space related not only to physical proximity but also to ownership and to mutual respect and trust.

Sharing agency. Devecchi discusses this in relation to power (the control we exert) and authority (social acceptance of that power). Teachers and TAs in her research study spoke of trusting each other to make decisions, and each being supportive of the other having a degree of independence in their work. However, this shared agency and independence contributed to a sense of interdependency that was essential for effective collaboration.

In the box on page 42 we have included some questions relating to these three aspects of sharing, to give you an opportunity to reflect on how they might apply to your own work setting.

Chapter summary

In this chapter we have provided an overview of some of the most recent and most important research relating to the work of TAs. The professional and academic literature relating to TAs is now extensive, reflecting the importance of the issues surrounding support staff and how schools can maximise the impact of their work. Literature and research relating to teachers and TAs working together is much less extensive, mirroring perhaps the lesser attention this topic receives in initial teacher training or ongoing professional development. TAs have been a topic of discussion for almost as long as we have had them in our schools. The recent research in the UK, however – which has to be recognised as world-leading – represents a huge step forwards, as it has provided us with fine details of TAs' work, and therefore shows much more clearly the way forward.

Bibliography

Alborz A., Pearson, D., Farrell, P. and Howes, A. (2009) The impact of adult support staff on pupils and mainstream schools. Technical Report. In *Research Evidence in Education Library*. London: EPPI-Centre, Social Science Research Unit, Institute of Education, University of London. Available at: http://eppi.ioe.ac.uk/cms/Default.aspx?tabid=2438 (accessed 20.4.15).

Blatchford, P., Bassett, P., Brown, P., Koutsoubou, M., Martin, C., Russell, A., Webster, R. with Rubie-Davies, C. (2009) *Deployment and Impact of Support Staff in Schools*. Research Report No DCSF-RR148. London: DCSF. Available at: www.ioe.ac.uk/DISS_Strand_2_Wave_2_Report.pdf (accessed 20.4.15).

Brown, J. and Harris, A. (2010) *Increased Expenditure on Associate Staff in schools and changes in student attainment*. London: TDA and SSAT. Available at: http://dera.ioe.ac.uk/10981 (accessed 20.4.15).

Cajkler W., Tennant G., Tiknaz Y., Sage, R., Tucker, S. and Taylor, C. (2007) A systematic literature review on how training and professional development activities impact on teaching assistants' classroom practice (1988–2006). In: *Research Evidence in Education Library*. London: EPPI-Centre, Social Science Research Unit, Institute of Education, University of London. Available at: http://eppi.ioe.ac.uk/cms/Default. aspx?tabid=2304 (accessed 20.4.15).

Department for Education and Skills (2002) *Time for Standards: Reforming the School Workforce*. London: DfES.

Devecchi, C. (2005) *Teachers and TAs Working Together in a Secondary School: Should we be Critical?* Paper presented at the British Educational Research Association Annual Conference, University of Glamorgan, 14–17 September.

Devecchi, C. and Brown, J. (2013, September) Perspectives on the 'preparedness' of teaching assistants: What gets in the way? Paper presented to British Educational Research Association (BERA) Annual Conference, University of Sussex, Brighton. Presented version available at: http://nectar.northampton.ac.uk/5712/ NECTAR.

Devecchi, C. and Rouse, M. (2010) An exploration of the features of effective collaboration between teachers and teaching assistants in secondary schools. *Support for Learning* 25 (2), 91–9.

Giangreco, M.F. and Broer, S. M. (2005) Questionable utilization of paraprofessionals in inclusive schools: Are we addressing symptoms or causes? *Focus on Autism and Other Developmental Disabilities*, 20, 10–26.

Giangreco, M.F., Doyle, M.B. and Suter, J.C. (2012) Constructively responding to requests for paraprofessionals: We keep asking the wrong questions. *Remedial and Special Education* 33 (06), pp. 362–373.

Radford, J., Bosanquet, P., Webster, R. and Blatchford, P. (2015) Scaffolding learning for independence: Clarifying teacher and teaching assistant roles for children with special educational needs. *Learning and Instruction* 36, 1–10.

Russell, A., Blatchford, P. and Webster, R. (2012) *Maximising the Impact of Teaching Assistants: Guidance for School Leaders and Teachers*. London: Routledge.

Stewart, J. (2009) *Classroom Assistants: Their Impact in Scottish Primary Schools*. Unpublished EdD thesis, University of Glasgow. Available at: http://theses.gla.ac.uk/1121.

Webster, R. and Blatchford, P. (2013). *The Making a Statement Project. Final Report. A Study of the Teaching and Support Experienced by Pupils with a Statement of Special Educational Needs in Mainstream Primary Schools*. London: University of London Institute of Education. Available at: www.nuffieldfoundation.org/ sites/default/files/files/mastreport.pdf (accessed 20.4.15).

Webster, R., Blatchford, P. and Russell, A. (2013) Challenging the role and deployment of teaching assistants in mainstream schools: The impact on schools. Final Report on the Effective Deployment of Teaching Assistants (EDTA) project. London: University of London Institute of Education. Available at: maximisingtas.co.uk/assets/content/edtareport-2.pdf (accessed 20.4.15).

Chapter 3

Before the lesson

This chapter begins the section of the book which deals with the very practical realities of what teachers and SENCOs can do to work more effectively with TAs on an everyday basis in the classroom. Framed in terms of *Before*, *During* and *After*, we look at the proactive strategies that are at your disposal, and under your control. You will not be surprised to see that this *Before* chapter is more substantial than the other two. You know that the best lessons have the best planning behind them. Even if you do not follow your lesson plan in every detail, the fact that you have planned carefully gives you a solid framework for the lesson with clear learning intentions for those students. You can then allow yourself some freedom, because you have given careful consideration beforehand to the lesson content and the teaching strategies you are going to use. But careful and thorough planning is always an essential element for successful teaching and learning.

Knowing this, before any pupils enter your classroom, you engage in the planning process: what you will teach across a term or half-term, and then each week; what resources you will need; how lesson periods will be divided up into different activities and content. You do this so that you can present a coherent and considered set of learning activities which will enable students to access content and concepts relating to your subject area and the prescribed curriculum. You also plan on the basis of students' age and abilities.

Even the most experienced teachers review their plans and intentions for upcoming lessons, and try to ensure that necessary resources are to hand. Resources are supports for your teaching:

- They facilitate student understanding (e.g. diagrams, 3-D models, case studies, video clips).
- They help to illustrate concepts (e.g. manipulatives in maths, models or demonstrations).
- They enable students to practise using new material you have taught (e.g. paper and pens, iPads and other technology, tools and materials).
- They quite simply provide tools for students to accomplish set tasks (e.g. stationery, IT, art materials, tools or equipment).

One of the resources available to you, and that you therefore need to plan for, is the TA who will be present in the lesson. Whether they accompany an individual student to your timetabled sessions or are assigned to your faculty or subject area, they represent an additional support for your teaching, to facilitate learning and understanding, help students practise new skills and knowledge, and help explain concepts. Assigning a TA to an individual student for a set number of hours each week (sometimes referred to as the Velcro model) is a decreasing trend given the new SEND Code of Practice in England, and its emphasis on all teachers being responsible for all of their students. We have also already referred to the recent research which strongly suggests that struggling students do not necessarily benefit from having the constant support of a TA.

One of the resources you need to plan for is the TA who will be present in the lessons. As with other resources, a TA can:

- facilitate student understanding – by repeating or re-phrasing what you have said, and linking new material to prior learning;
- help to illustrate concepts, by presenting material in a slightly different way or by using additional, differentiated resources;
- enable students to practise using new material you have taught, giving the student the extra time and support they may need to work successfully and independently.

So in this chapter we offer suggestions on four areas relating to what you can do to prepare and plan *before* the TA comes into your classroom. Initially you may not know who the TA is going to be, but as long as you know when you will have a TA to support your lessons, you can plan ahead for what you would wish her to do. As you consider the suggestions we make, keep in mind the question that we asked in the Introduction: *What is it that you want from your TA?* The answer to that question should drive the decisions you make about what you want the TA to actually do as you plan your lessons.

Before the lesson

1. Know why the pupils are receiving support from the TA.
2. Ensure that the TAs have access to the medium-term plans at the start of the scheme of work (SOW).
3. Plan ahead for the tasks the TA will complete during the lesson.
4. Plan ahead for how the TA will be involved in managing behaviour.

What Makes an Outstanding Ofsted Lesson (SecEd, 2012) states that one of the key points that sets apart an outstanding lesson from one that is good or satisfactory includes:

> The use of resources, *including the use of teaching assistants where applicable*, [to] promote rapid learning for pupils regardless of their aptitudes and needs. (emphasis added)

Know why pupils are receiving support from the TA

As part of the process of differentiating instruction to meet individual student needs, a teacher needs to know what those student needs are, and the particular need that has been identified that justifies support from a TA. Why does the student have an adult shadowing them to lessons? Does this only happen in your lessons? Or is this a constant for the student throughout the day? What type of support is the TA assigned to provide for the student? If the TA is assigned to your faculty, subject area, or even classroom, what is her brief? Why was it considered necessary to have her there? Is her work supposed to have a particular focus? Or is she entirely at your disposal, to assign as you see fit?

Here are some aspects to consider:

- **Check the school intranet for the student's record.**

  The record-keeping database on the school intranet should include information about a student that will clarify why a TA has been allocated. The record should enable you to become more familiar with the student's strengths and areas of need. Both of these are important: knowledge of strengths that you can build or draw upon; knowledge of areas of need so that you can assess whether the student is likely to be able to access the proposed curriculum and associated activities. This knowledge will help inform your planning so that that student is fully included in the lessons; it should also help you to better understand why a TA has been assigned.

- **Be aware of the relevance of IEP targets to your curriculum area.**

  If the student has an IEP (Individual Education Plan), IBP (Individual Behaviour Plan) or Education Health and Care Plan (EHCP) as they are now referred to in England, there will be specific targets for student progress. There may well be reference to the significance of the targets to particular curriculum areas. You will find more details of what may be included in the plan on the next page. An important consideration will be the student's level of literacy, for which we have also provided some guidance in the following box.

Think literacy

All targets for student learning and behaviour are important but some of the most crucial will be those relating to literacy and numeracy. These are basic skills, without which students will struggle with many curriculum areas and activities, particularly those with a high literacy or numeracy content (e.g. history, geography, technology). The language content of secondary maths lessons also presents difficulties for many students.

So as you plan ahead for how you will differentiate to make your lesson more accessible to all students, consider:

- the language content and difficulty of any resources you are planning to use (the level of difficulty of the questions you plan to ask, including the use of open-ended, opinion-type questions);
- the need for 'thinking time' (which we address further in the next chapter) so that students can process information; students who have difficulty processing language will need to process both the questions you ask and the answers they give;
- key vocabulary which may need to be presented to students and rehearsed until they are familiar enough with it to use it in a meaningful way;
- alternative means of assessment or of students showing their understanding (e.g., oral rather than written presentations) if literacy levels hamper the student demonstrating the full extent of his or her understanding.

Individualised plans

When a student is experiencing difficulties, we need to identify what those difficulties are, decide on some appropriate action, carry out that action, then review its effectiveness. However, a whole industry has grown up around designing templates, creating targets, measuring progress – and generally stressing over the paperwork. Some SENCOs have literally made themselves ill in the process.

The test of a good plan is whether a teacher knows about a student's difficulties, plans accordingly, and differentiates effectively in the classroom, science lab, studio, or gym, rather than the plan being used only by the TA running a small group intervention.

The plan should be a working document, useful to all staff who work with the pupil. It should be constantly at hand; its design should allow for regular updates and comments by TAs, teachers and parents. In some schools, an extra sheet is attached to the IEP for daily/weekly updates, rather than waiting for a scheduled annual review, which makes much more sense in many ways.

Here are some important points to note about effective individualised plans.

- They should only contain what is *additional to and different from* the school's differentiated curriculum planning for all students.
- They should include three or four SMART short-term targets which have been set through discussion with the pupil and parents. Being:
  - Specific
  - Measurable
  - Attainable
  - Relevant
  - Time constrained

  is what makes the targets 'smart'. But it also means that anyone can see when each one has been met.
- Targets should be expressed in jargon-free language and clearly understandable for all concerned – not least the pupil himself/herself, who should be able to say 'Today I hit one of my targets … I was able to write the date/complete a section of the workbook/spell three key words linked to subject/able to ask a question…'
- They should describe the child's strengths as well as areas for development.
- Teaching and behaviour management strategies should be described with details of who will deliver them, when and where.
- Necessary additional resources should be listed.
- There should be a date for review, with the names of those involved in reviewing.

There have been moves to minimise the number of IEPs and other formal types of individualised plan. Many schools now use more general 'provision mapping' as a way of allocating different types of support to individuals.

© 2016, *Achieving Outstanding Classroom Support in Your Secondary School*, J. Morgan, C. Jones and S. Booth-Coates, Routledge

- **Talk to relevant specialists, e.g. SENCO, or the TA.**

The SENCO is the designated specialist in the school for special or additional learning needs, and will be able to provide (or direct you to) resources and information relating to the types of difficulties some of your students may encounter. The SENCO should also be able to fill you in on the needs of specific students. Another relevant designated specialist may be the Speech and Language Therapist. Now we can almost hear you say, 'I haven't time to be running around the school trying to talk to these people about all the students who come to my classes with a TA!' but don't forget that the TA assigned to the student may actually be something of an expert on the student's particular difficulty. She may have supported that student for some time, or she may have worked with a similar student in the past. So she may well be familiar with the individual student's strengths and needs, as well as with general principles of effective practice relating to that type of need. She may also have attended training relating to that type of difficulty, and may therefore have more generally useful information and suggestions to offer. She comes to you – on a regular basis! – so we recommend that you put her knowledge to good use. This will also add to her sense of being valued, as we discuss in the *After* chapter.

As a SENCO...

You are likely to be the person who knows best why a particular student has been allocated support from a TA, and what that student's particular needs, strengths and targets are. So you will need to ensure the following:

1. If a supporting TA is assigned, she will be well informed – she will know enough about the student's IEP targets to provide focused support, and know enough about the student's strengths to help the student use them to access the curriculum. And she will know enough about the student's condition or disability that she can respond appropriately to the student's behaviour.
2. Teachers whose classes the TA will attend to support pupils will have some idea of the students' needs and areas of difficulty.
3. The teachers with whom the TA will work will have some idea of the TA's levels of knowledge, understanding and experience – in relation to the curriculum area and in relation to the specific challenges of the students she is assigned to support.
4. Staff are informed as early as possible when TAs are absent from school and or otherwise unable to attend their classes, as teachers will have planned lessons based on being able to use their TA and parts of the lesson may not be able to go ahead without additional support for the planned activities.

Ensure that the TAs have access to the medium-term plans at the start of the Scheme of Work (SOW)

A TA who does not know how her role fits into the instructional plans for the term, week, or even the lesson, is like a person who is placed in the middle of a game and is expected to help her team win when she has no idea of the rules. What action should she take to be helpful? What actions would be unhelpful? What constitutes winning in this game? What constitutes 'losing'? How will she know which one she is contributing to? In some cases, she may not really know which 'side' she is on – is she part of the 'student' team or part of the 'teacher' team? And of course, for each classroom where she supports a student, the 'game' may feel different, as she has to work with different teachers, whose expectations may not be the same, and different students.

Your TA will be best equipped to support you and the students if she has a clear idea beforehand of which aspects of the curriculum are to be studied in the coming weeks and months. Otherwise she is working in the dark and has no chance to think ahead, no sense of where her work fits with the general plan.

- **Make the SOW accessible on the school network for TAs to look through.**

  If the Scheme of Work is available on the school intranet, in theory a TA could access it that way. In some schools it is a requirement to post Schemes of Work. You would need to be sure that all SOWs are up to date and stored where they are readily accessible. At a later stage you will need to check that the TA has actually been able to access the relevant SOW. But even if plans for specific lessons or activities are not available, the general outline Scheme of Work will provide a useful overview for your TA.

- **Each teacher to make a hard copy of the SOW accessible.**

  Hard copy of the SOW can easily be kept in your classroom in a designated place where the TA can access it without interrupting you or your work. If it were pinned to a classroom notice board or kept in a folder, she could check it as often as needed, returning it to the designated place at the end of the lesson or when she has finished looking at it. You can decide whether to offer her a print copy of it if she would prefer that. We cannot emphasise enough the importance of a TA knowing what she is supposed to be supporting in terms of curriculum content and development of student skills. If you want her to contribute to 'winning the game', she needs to know how she can best do that.

- **Consider inviting the TA to departmental/faculty planning meetings.**

  With the approval of the Head of Department or Faculty, a TA could be invited to departmental/ faculty planning meetings, at least once per term. This would probably be most helpful at the beginning of the term, as it would serve as a means of communicating curriculum plans and expectations to the TA, and of possibly gaining insight into how the curriculum could be made more accessible to more students. An experienced TA may have many useful suggestions to offer, based on her work with current and previous students, as well as current and previous teachers. These suggestions can be useful for a wide range of students, not just those allocated support. They may derive from good practice she has seen in other departments or faculties in the school. So before she even comes into your classroom, you could advocate for her attending departmental or faculty meetings.

As a SENCO...

1. It would be advisable for you to meet with TAs on a regular basis. This will allow you to pass important information to the TAs, as well as checking that there are no unresolved issues or timetabling difficulties. These meetings may have to take place during school hours, unless the TAs are paid to work extra hours at the beginning or end of the school day. If there is no such arrangement for additional hours, you will need to negotiate taking TAs off timetable for these short periods of time, as it represents an investment in increasing their levels of effectiveness. It is certainly justifiable with the move away from specified hours of constant TA support for individual students.

2. If necessary you could advocate for TAs to be invited to departmental/faculty meetings at least once per term – for the reasons described above. For the TAs who are assigned to a single faculty or department this would be fairly simple. Where they work across faculties, you may need to help them decide where their presence would be most useful, and consider which of the faculty or departmental meetings would benefit them most.

Plan ahead for the tasks the TA will complete during the lesson

As you plan specific lesson content and structure you need to:

*   Know when TA support will be timetabled for your lessons.
*   Work with the SENCO to develop plans that will focus on meeting the needs of the students rather than the constraints of the timetable or scheme of work – let your work be need-led rather than topic-led.
*   Consider how you can build a positive working relationship with the TA.

Know when TA support will be timetabled. Knowing when you will have the support of a TA will enable you to plan ahead more efficiently. Just the presence of an extra adult will allow you to plan different types of groupings or activities that would be more difficult if you were working alone. You will have an extra pair of hands and eyes for monitoring group work or individual work; you could work with a small group of students while the majority of the class work independently, with the TA roving to provide assistance. In short, once you know when a TA will be working in your classroom, you can expand your thinking into more diverse methods of engaging students in learning activities.

Work with the SENCO to meet the needs of the student rather than the timetable. So much of what we do in secondary schools is determined by the demands of the timetable. And much of it is absolutely necessary, to avoid chaos in an organisation as large as a secondary school; and in terms of steady student progress towards learning goals, including formal examinations and other assessments. However, it is easy to forget that schools exist for individual students rather than students en masse, or for the general achievement of academic qualifications. Working with the SENCO you can identify best practice ways of deploying the TA so as to better meet individual student needs, in addition to meeting the needs of your school and curricular schedules.

The Welsh government publication *Becoming a Qualified Teacher: Handbook of Guidance* (DCELLS, 2009) states that the effectiveness of teaching and learning can be increased when "teachers and other adults work together when both planning and interacting with learners. Additional adults are increasingly making a valuable contribution to learners' knowledge, skills and understanding, and their deployment needs to be planned so that support for individual learners and groups of learners can be targeted effectively and efficiently."

Consider how you can build a positive working relationship with the TA. Plan for how you will find out the strengths of the TAs who work in your classroom so that you can better use them to support the delivery of the lesson. You obviously cannot do this for each TA at the beginning of the term, but you could work slowly through the TAs assigned to your students or classroom. You might ask the TA to list or describe their areas of expertise on a simple slip of paper. Or you could ask the SENCO if this information could be gathered more centrally and distributed to relevant teachers.

- **Decide where the student assigned a TA's support will sit in the classroom.**

  If you have students for whom individual TA support is considered necessary, be determined not to have a designated TA chair, or to always have the supported student sitting on the periphery of the class. Decide where it would be both convenient and inclusive to position the TA and assigned student. Having an adult sitting among students, you would not want her to block access to areas of the classroom or students' sight of the whiteboard or other area of focus; you would not want her to be so conspicuous that it would add to the student's possible embarrassment at being 'minded' by a TA. But the most typical spot for a TA supporting a single student is probably at the back of the class and edge of the group – almost out of the picture. So try to avoid having that happen by planning ahead for where she might sit and be part of the group.

- **Ask yourself whether the best use of the TA is to have her always sit with the student.**

  Over the years, we have come to assume that attaching a TA to a struggling student is a good thing, because the student is not then left to struggle alone or unnoticed. But ask yourself:

  - Would it improve the student's independence (and self-esteem) to be allowed to work alone for some of the lesson?
  - Could other students benefit from the TA circulating and helping more generally?

  In your planning for the lesson (and for what you will assign the TA to do during the lesson) consider the extent to which you could change the typical pattern of work for the TA – and for yourself – so as to extend the potential benefits of having the TA's help, beyond just minding one student. We need to ensure that we are challenging the student, providing respectful and engaging tasks to move the student on to succeed and reach his or her full potential. But that does not have to translate into constant supervision by the TA.

- **Consider what mechanism you could use to garner feedback from the TA to support the student's progress.**

  Included in your planning will be mechanisms for assessing how well students have understood what you have taught. You will have planned to ask questions, provide quizzes or written exercises to make these assessments, or set homework. With the addition of a TA to your classroom, you can now consider how she could contribute to this process of assessment. But this too will need forward planning, otherwise it is unlikely to happen. Consider:

  - Would you and she have time during the day to discuss her work and how the students she has supported have responded to the teaching activities you have provided?
  - Could you meet directly after the lesson or would it be better at another point during her paid work time?
  - If you are unable to meet together, could you ask her to use sticky notes or other written means of communicating her observations?
  - Could you devise a simple feedback sheet that she could use as she works with students?
  - What type of information would you like her to provide as feedback to you?

  We have provided a simple pro forma that you could consider using to garner feedback from your TA. You will find it at the back of the book. Copies of this pro forma could be kept in a designated folder where the TA can access them as she enters the room, and deposit them as she leaves.

Safeguard? Or Bodyguard?

TAs are employed in schools to safeguard students and provide them with better access to the curriculum and higher potential success. Their employment in such large numbers has been supported by the argument for greater inclusion in schools. However, Michael Giangreco, Mary Beth Doyle and Jesse Suter (2012), researchers from New England, have questioned the traditional use of TAs to support individual pupils, suggesting that there are "inadvertent detrimental effects associated with overreliance on paraprofessionals" (the term used for TAs in the United States). They suggest that these include:

- unnecessary dependence on the TA;

- interference with teacher engagement – where the TA is offering support, the teacher is much less likely to interact with the student;

- limited access to competent instruction, as the TA may not have particularly well-developed teaching skills and may have only limited subject knowledge;

- interference with peer interactions, as support is most likely to be one-to-one;

- stigmatisation, as students may resent being singled out as needy and object to being so closely monitored by an adult.

Gill Richards and Felicity Armstrong (2008, p. 124), researchers in the UK, describe TAs as 'bodyguards' to students (especially those with challenging behaviour) and point out that their presence could be seen as a barrier to inclusion, as the supported student is segregated from the rest of the class by his or her TA as much as by his or her behaviour.

- **Adjust your planning sheet to include the question:** *How will the TA support be used in this lesson?*

As you write down the support you need on your planning sheets or lesson plans, putting the TA to good use will become a more automatic and natural part of your planning. But it might help if you amend the pro forma you currently use to include this question as a prompt. If your school provides the pro forma, you may want to give feedback to your department head or to the SENCO that this element would be a useful addition to remind all staff of the need to plan for how TAs will be included in lessons.

- **Plan to talk to your TA to ensure she is comfortable in carrying out the required tasks.**

As part of the process of making the TA feel that she is welcome in your classroom, you can plan to seek out her views on the tasks you wish to assign to her. Make a note to do this: to ask her whether she would feel comfortable doing certain tasks as opposed to others. And by 'comfortable' we mean 'able' (sufficiently knowledgeable/skilled) and willing. You need to let her know that you would prefer her to tell you if she feels she does not have the necessary knowledge or skills to support students in your curriculum area. This is better than her not telling you, and the student therefore not receiving the necessary support.

- **Consider what the TA will be concentrating on in each section of the lesson.**

  As you plan the different segments of a lesson, consider what it would be most useful for the TA to be engaged in doing. Bear these points in mind:

  - When you are presenting important new information or instructions to students for an activity, the TA needs to be present and receiving the same information or instructions so that she knows what is expected of the student and can reinforce your requirements. Sending her out of the class to make copies or deliver messages while you introduce topics or give students instructions means that she misses essential information that some students will need repeated.
  - Where there are tasks which you will ask students to complete independently, the TA may be used to circulate and help more generally, instead of sitting next to the assigned student. That student may be a priority for the TA, but support is better given intermittently if the student is to learn to work independently.
  - During independent tasks, if the TA is circulating to provide more general support, you will have more access to the supported student and therefore will be able to give him/her the benefit of your subject expertise more easily.

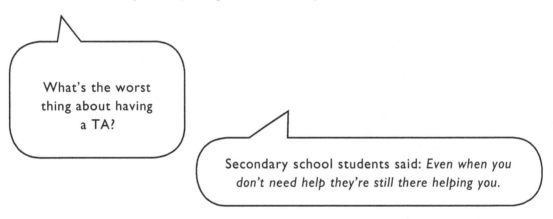

As a SENCO...

1. Work with subject teachers and TAs to provide training so that staff are aware of the skills and expertise of TAs and the TAs understand the tasks required. As a SENCO, this is a point at which you really can influence effectiveness, as you carefully consider support needs alongside the current knowledge and skills of your TAs. What needs to be done? Which of your TAs has the knowledge and skills to do it? If you do not have a TA skilled enough for the assignment, what can be done to upskill someone? And who would be the most appropriate person? Is this something that you can do yourself? Or will you need support from an external agency, such as the local authority? These are questions that need to be addressed as you balance support needs against available human resources. You may wish to conduct an audit of the skills and knowledge of the TAs who come under your direction, as an aid to answering these questions.
2. Keep the TAs up to date with any data that has significance to their role. In primary school settings TAs are quite often assigned to collect data, but this may be less common in secondary settings. The implication is that TAs may not be accustomed to the idea of data- or evidence-based decision-making.
3. Provide information relating to pupils if it affects their ability to access the curriculum – this is important for teachers and TAs.

4. Make sure IEPs and Education & Health Care plans are up to date, so that teachers and TAs have access to the most recent version on the school intranet.

Plan ahead for how the TA will be involved in managing behaviour

Managing behaviour is on everyone's list of responsibilities when they work in a school – by default, even if it is not specified on a job description. As you are all too well aware, if you do not manage the students' behaviour, they will willingly take over and manage yours! Among a TA's responsibilities in your classroom is the responsibility to support appropriate behaviour (and deal – where necessary – with inappropriate behaviour). So as you include the TA in your planning, consider:

*   What are your behavioural expectations? (What constitutes acceptable and unacceptable behaviour in your classroom? What behaviours will you tolerate to a reasonable extent? What behaviours will you absolutely not tolerate under any circumstances? Are students expected to largely work silently? Or will you tolerate a low buzz of conversation? To what extent are students allowed to move around the room? Do you insist on hands up to ask questions or provide answers?) Although there will be general school-wide expectations for student behaviour, you will have a certain amount of leeway in your classroom. What are the points on which you may choose to relax expectations – and under what circumstances? To what extent will you allow the TA to also relax those expectations?
*   What are your preferred strategies for managing student behaviour? (Are you a minimalist, preferring 'The Look' to a fuss? Do you make a determined effort to emphasise positive behaviour and try to ignore the negative unless it really gets in the way of your teaching and student learning? Or do you believe in keeping very strict control over behaviour, allowing students no room for interpreting your expectations? What will you expect the TA to do?)
*   How will you convey this to the TAs who work in your classroom? Consistency of approach, as you know, is considered an essential element for effective management of behaviour, so how will you ensure this type of consistency between you and the TA? Your TA will need to know a) what you expect from the students, and b) what you expect from her. How will you communicate this to her? As a written overview? In a brief introductory chat? Or just by waiting to see how she manages and correcting misapprehensions only as they arise?

As we have already stated, working together as a team is vitally important if you have a challenging pupil or class! Both you and the TA need to be familiar with the school behaviour policy and how that relates to the classroom. There needs to be rules, rights and responsibilities clearly displayed for all to see and refer to, and ideally these should also be discussed with the pupils so they feel ownership of them. All staff in the classroom need to know them so that they can refer to them when responding to inappropriate behaviour. '*What does our rule say about...?*' Proactive and Reactive plans need to be put in place. If there are particularly challenging students in the class, discussions should have taken place with parents, the SENCO and the TA and a plan should be drawn up to ensure there is consistency of approach. A proactive plan will include strategies that staff, parents and pupils will use in order to prevent the challenging behaviour; for example, providing work at the appropriate level, sitting away from distractions or providing a reward system just for the pupil to encourage compliant behaviour. The Reactive plan will include actions that the teacher and TA will carry out when an incident occurs. Too often when there is an incident all adults in the area descend on the pupil, and this intensity of attention means that the student must win in the eyes of his peers – which leads to an escalation of confrontation! Deciding ahead of time who will deal with the behaviour and who will maintain order and focus for the rest of the class will help to minimise the impact of the behaviour for all students.

As a SENCO...

1. Ensure that TAs know the school behaviour policy. Many TAs do not even know where to look for a copy, even though it should be readily available for anyone to consult.
2. Provide training for TAs in general behavioural strategies and also on the uniqueness of dealing with pupils with autism, ADHD, etc. who may not respond in the same way as other students do to rewards and sanctions.
3. Ensure that Proactive and Reactive plans are in place for pupils and if restraint is likely to be required for particular students, that staff have attended appropriate training.

Northern Ireland's 2005–6 report of school inspections, *Effective Use of Assistants for Pupils with Special Educational Needs in Mainstream Schools* (Education & Training Inspectorate (N. Ireland), 2006), remarked that Classroom Assistants (CAs) who supported students with special needs were most effective when the CA worked closely in partnership with a teacher. But the report also pointed out that the teacher needed to a) plan well for the CA's role in the lessons and b) make arrangements for obtaining feedback from the CA on student learning and behaviour.

The report noted that when CAs were poorly briefed, or had poor subject knowledge, they focused more on task completion than on developing students' skills, understanding or independence.

Ofsted's 2015 *Handbook for Inspecting Schools in England* states that Inspectors must evaluate the use of and contribution made by Teaching Assistants. They should consider whether Teaching Assistants are clear about their role and knowledgeable about the pupils they support. They should also consider how well the school ensures that Teaching Assistants have sufficient knowledge of the subjects in which they provide support.

In Wales the DCELLS 2010 research on implementation of the *National Agreement* included the comment that "TAs were keen to emphasise that their roles were distinct from those of teaching staff. They were concerned that they should not be deployed to undertake work that should be done by teacher."

Chapter summary

In this chapter we have been considering some of the steps you can take in preparation for having a TA work with you in your classroom. We acknowledge that you may not have received guidance or preparation for this supervisory role – either in your initial training or since – and thus we have provided quite detailed suggestions for how you can approach the work it entails. Some of the suggestions are for minor actions on your part; others will take more time and preparation. But the purpose here is to help you think through how you might best use the support of a TA, rather than waiting until she comes into your classroom, perhaps feeling uncertain about what she actually does during your lessons, and whether that is actually benefitting any of the students in real terms. Ultimately, we hope you would get to a point where you are automatically planning for the TA's contribution as part of your normal planning. But expect this to take some time. It represents a real change for most teachers in what they see as their role, and how they approach their planning.

Before the lesson: summary of suggestions

1. Know why pupils are receiving support from the TA.
    *   Check the school intranet for the pupil's record.
    *   Be aware of the relevance of IEP targets to your curriculum area.
    *   Talk to relevant specialists, e.g. TA, SENCO, TA.

2. Ensure that the TAs have access to the medium-term plans at the start of the Scheme of Work (SOW).
    *   Make the SOW accessible on the school network for TAs to look through.
    *   Each department to make a hard copy of the SOW accessible.
    *   Invite the TA to departmental planning meetings.

3. Plan ahead for the tasks the TA will complete during the lesson.
    *   Know when TA support will be timetabled for your lessons.
    *   Work with the SENCO to meet the needs of the student rather than the timetable – let the work be need-led rather than topic-led.
    *   Consider how you can build a positive working relationship with the TA.
    *   Decide where the student assigned a TA's support will sit in the classroom.
    *   Ask yourself whether the best use of the TA is to have her always sit with the student.
    *   Consider what mechanism you could use to garner feedback from the TA to support the student's progress.
    *   Adjust your planning sheet to include the question: How will the TA support be used in this lesson?
    *   Make time to talk to the TA to ensure they are comfortable in carrying out the task.
    *   Consider what the TA will be concentrating on in each section of the lesson.

4. Plan ahead for how the TA will be involved in managing behaviour.
    *   What are your behavioural expectations?
    *   What are your preferred strategies for managing student behaviour?
    *   How will you convey this to the TAs who work in your classroom?

Bibliography

Bentham, S. and Hutchins, R. (2012) *Improving Pupil Motivation Together: Teachers and Teaching Assistants Working Collaboratively*. London: Routledge.

Blatchford, P., Russell, A. and Webster, R. (2011) *Reassessing the Impact of Teaching Assistants: How Research Challenges Practice and Policy*. London: Routledge.

DCELLS (2009) *Becoming a Qualified Teacher: Handbook of Guidance*. Guidance Circular No: 017/2009. Cardiff: WAG.

DCELLS. (2010) *Research into the National Agreement on Raising Standards and Tackling Workloads*. Cardiff: Welsh Government.

Education and Training Inspectorate (N. Ireland) (2006) *Effective Use of Assistants for Pupils with Special Educational Needs in Mainstream Schools*. Report of an Inspection survey, 2005–6. Belfast: ETI (NI).

Giangreco, M.F. and Broer, S.M. (2005) Questionable utilization of paraprofessionals in inclusive schools: Are we addressing symptoms or causes? *Focus on Autism and Other Developmental Disabilities*, 20, 10–26.

Giangreco, M.F., Doyle, M.B. and Suter, J.C. (2012) Constructively responding to requests for paraprofessionals: We keep asking the wrong questions. *Remedial and Special Education* 33 (06), pp. 362–373.

Richards, G. and Armstrong, F. (2008) *Key Issues for Teaching Assistants Working in Diverse and Inclusive Schools*. London: Routledge.

SecEd (2012) *What Makes an Outstanding Ofsted Lesson*. Available at: www.sec-ed.co.uk/best-practice/what-makes-an-outstanding-ofsted-lesson (accessed 17.7.15).

Chapter 4

During the lesson

In the last chapter we looked at strategies you could use to prepare for having a TA work in your classroom as part of your forward planning. We recommended that you begin to include TAs as part of your lesson planning, under the heading of resources and to support differentiation. You well know that careful planning does not guarantee perfect lessons, because things can go wrong, discussions can get side-tracked, students can get bored or disruptive. But thorough planning does set your classroom up for success. So now you are ready for your classes – and the accompanying TA(s). In this chapter we make suggestions for what you can do during class to make most effective use of the TA support allocated to your students, under the following two headings.

During the lesson

1. Involve TAs in all parts of the lesson.
2. Include TAs in the ongoing/formative assessment process during the lesson.

As you consider these suggestions, we would remind you again of that crucial question: *What is it that I want from my TA?* What do I expect of her? (not merely, what you expect her to do, but what is the purpose of having her in your classroom). Thus as you decide how to incorporate these suggestions into your teaching, you should essentially be evaluating whether your decisions will contribute to helping you achieve what you want from your TA.

Involve TAs in all parts of the lesson

- **Observe basic courtesies.**

  This may seem like an insignificant suggestion, but sadly, many TAs have told us that they enter, work through and leave some lessons without being addressed by the teacher at all. Surely no one is too busy to extend the courtesy of a quick 'hello' or eye-contact and a smile, so that the TA's presence is acknowledged. The TA is, after all, part of the instructional team, part of the classroom dynamic. If she is invisible, the chances are the student she supports is also off your radar. We are not suggesting a prolonged conversation that would interfere with settling your students and starting the lesson – simply an exchange of greetings as the TA enters the classroom. As we work with TAs, we always encourage them to do the same – to act more like a member of the classroom team so that teachers are more likely to treat them that way.

- **Give the TA specific targets for their work, e.g. a certain group/individual/focus.**

  You have already considered this in your planning, so this is a reminder to make sure you convey your clear expectations to the TA.

  - What is it that you want her to do during this lesson?
  - Who should she be working with?
  - What outcomes are you hoping for?

  You may choose to provide this information via a sheet of instructions, or a quick exchange of ideas once the class is settled. You may have a standard format or set of expectations which apply to the majority of your lessons. As you and your TA become more used to collaborating more closely, a routine can develop so that the TA knows whether to check a folder for instructions when she comes into the classroom, or wait for your verbal instructions. If you follow a standard set of procedures in all your classes, then the TA knows she can set to work straight away, and will only expect instructions from you if you are making changes to the usual routine.

- **Provide prompt sheets to support the TA's work with an individual student, e.g. questions they could ask pupils, differentiated outcomes.**

  As you plan for a particular class session, you may jot down questions you intend to ask students, or aspects of the topic you need to mention. If you have a TA in your classroom during that lesson and she is assigned to work with an individual student or a small group, it would be important to ensure that the students working with her have access to the same information and skills development activities. Consider whether your personal prompt sheet could simply be photocopied and passed to the TA, or printed from the computer if you have it in electronic format. Then as she works with the individual student (or small group that includes the supported/ allocated student), you know that group or individual student will get the same subject coverage and extension of thinking as the rest of the class while you work with them.

  A March 2015 guidance document – *Making Best Use of Teaching Assistants* – from the Education Endowment Fund (EEF) makes the following seven recommendations:

  1. TAs should not be used as an informal teaching resource for low-attaining pupils.
  2. Use TAs to add value to what teachers do, not replace them.
  3. Use TAs to help pupils develop independent learning skills and manage their own learning.
  4. Ensure TAs are fully prepared for their role in the classroom.
  5. Use TAs to deliver high-quality one-to-one and small group support using structured interventions.
  6. Adopt evidence-based interventions to support TAs in their small group and one-to-one instruction.
  7. Ensure explicit connections are made between learning from everyday classroom teaching and structured interventions.

  Note this last recommendation – that direct links be made between the work directed by the class teacher and any activities directed by a TA for a group or individual. This helps to ensure that all students access the same curriculum, and that students who struggle understand that their work with the TA is not a separate activity, but is part of what the rest of the class are doing, and part of the teacher's overall instructional plan.

Too often there is not enough linkage between intervention support and general class work – it may in fact not even link at all! We are not suggesting that the work should always be the same but that definite links are made. For example, if the lesson is Geography then the TA may work from the Literacy and Numeracy framework (LNF) and incorporate the relevant literacy or numeracy skills into the Geography session. The TA may use the IEP/EHCP targets and strategies which will work alongside the lesson objectives; for example, writing about volcanoes but highlighting capital letters, punctuation. And if the student goes to another room for intervention with the TA, there must be a seamless transition, so that when they return to the lesson, they can re-take their seat knowing what is expected of them. These intervention groups may be taken by the TA or yourself to communicate to the pupils that you are concerned about their progress as well as the progress of the majority of the class.

- **Work with a group, e.g. not always the SEN/ targeted students.**

As a qualified teacher, you are the expert in both curriculum content and pedagogy, or teaching strategies. So you really are best placed to support all students in developing understanding of the content and concepts relating to your particular curriculum area. At secondary level, where subject content becomes much more specialised, there are usually key concepts that your students need to grasp. Your TA may not be an expert in either curriculum or pedagogy. If you sometimes allocate the TA to general supervisory duties as the class completes an assigned task, you will be freed up to work with a small group of students who may be struggling. Switching roles with the TA in this way will give you an opportunity to better understand the difficulties some students experience with your curriculum area, and it will give the students the benefit of your particular expertise – and enthusiasm – for the subject area. You may have planned to do this beforehand, or you may decide to switch roles with the TA on an ad hoc basis, as you see a need arise.

> A 2002 survey produced by the University of Warwick Institute of Education for the National Union of Teachers (NUT) referred to face-to-face work with students as "the most pleasurable aspect of the teachers' job" and suggested that if this is delegated to TAs, potential teachers may choose to be TAs instead of teachers! (See Neill, 2002.)

The TA cannot be an expert in every subject the student is timetabled to attend – perhaps she has expertise in none of them. Her expertise lies in supporting struggling students. This type of support could benefit other students in the class and your expertise in the subject area can benefit the students the TA supports who struggle with learning in general. Supported students may also welcome the break from the constant supervision of a TA. Remember, no mainstream student should need help all of the time.

We asked secondary school students: *What do you think TAs do? What is their job?*

They said: *I don't think they just help the children I think they're the teacher's right hand man, doing all the extra bits for the teacher.*

Authors Karen Vincett, Hilary Cremin and Gary Thomas in their 2005 book *Teachers and Assistants Working Together* propose three approaches to effective team working in classrooms. These are designed for primary school classrooms but are worth considering for secondary school settings. They are:

- *Room Management,* where one of the adults is designated the Learning Manager and works intensively with a small group of students, and the other adult is designated the Activity Manager and supervises the work of the rest of the class.

- *Zoning,* where the classroom is divided into zones or activity areas and each of the adults has responsibility for specific 'geographic' zones. Either the teacher or the TA can take on the role of the Learning Manager or the Activity Manager, and the assignment of zones should be balanced according to the activities taking place and the need for support in each of the zones. So essentially these two approaches relate to clear role distinctions, and the adults are working independently.

- *Reflective Teamwork,* their third approach, is as the name suggests more collaborative, and their recommendations are based on 15 minutes of daily collaborative planning and reflection.

This is not likely to be feasible in a secondary school where multiple TAs pass through a classroom during the day. An uninterrupted 15 minutes may not be possible even in a classroom where a TA is assigned for longer portions of the day or week. But all three approaches are worth considering in principle.

As a SENCO...

1. Consider the point made above about teachers' prompt or planning sheets being copied for TAs to use, especially in relation to questions the teacher will ask students. It would be a good idea to provide training for all TAs on effective questioning techniques, so they will generally be better equipped to support increased learning, participation and engagement as well as raising student self-esteem. This is particularly important in light of the research we reported in the earlier chapter, which showed that TAs tend not to use the kind of open questions which require deeper thinking on the part of the students.
2. Consider how you can provide training for TAs to work with particular intervention groups. Again, the research shows that – unsurprisingly – TAs are most likely to be effective in their work when they are assigned to provide very structured, focused interventions.
3. Monitor progress of intervention groups and don't be afraid to change schemes and arrangements if they are shown not to improve pupil progress. Use the evidence to make decisions which will provide greater benefit to students and make better use of TAs' time and talents.
4. Encourage TAs to comment on students' progress towards their IEP targets so that progress can be seen and celebrated at reviews.

What's the worst thing about having a TA?

Secondary school students said: *They sit next to you all the time like a shadow.*

Include TAs in the ongoing/formative assessment process during the lesson

Formative assessment – the ongoing process of monitoring student understanding so as to inform your teaching – allows you to make adjustments as necessary during the lesson to accommodate student needs. It also allows you to better plan for upcoming lessons, as you base your planning on formative assessment data. We would suggest that TAs can provide you with support for that formative assessment in the following ways:

- **Encourage TAs to feed back on learning outcomes and pupil responses to tasks.**

  Once the TA is familiar with the learning outcomes for a lesson period, she should be able to give you feedback on a student's achievements in relation to those outcomes during the lesson period, noting areas of particular success or difficulty. The way in which you obtain such information from her will be determined by your work schedules and timetables. If there is no time for a conversation as one class leaves and the next arrives, you can set up a system where the TA leaves notes for you – using a feedback pro forma as suggested in the previous section, or by making entries in a log (see box).

  > John Hattie, author of the 2009 publication *Visible Learning*, in which he reports the results of a meta-analysis of over 800 research studies into the influences on school achievement, has concluded that "the most powerful single influence enhancing achievement is feedback".

  You should also check whether the TA knows the marking policy of the school (and/or your preferences for marking work). Are TAs allowed to write in student books or make written comments on their work, as a means of providing feedback? Or would you prefer that she only provides feedback to you directly? The 'correct' way to mark students' work can be quite a controversial topic. If you use Assessment for Learning in the school, has the TA had training in the principles and practices of AfL? How will you have her communicate to you what she has discovered about student learning through using AfL processes?

The Teacher–TA log

Some teacher–TA teams who have difficulty finding a time to meet and discuss student progress or concerns use a log where each jots down brief pieces of information – rather like a home–school record. The teacher may leave a note for the TA, to focus her attention on a certain aspect of the lesson which she would like dealt with in a particular way, or to notify her of a change in what was originally planned. The TA may be asked to leave a brief note about how a student she supports managed during class, and whether there were any difficulties, etc.

If the log is left in a specific place, the TA can collect it at the beginning of the lesson, check what the teacher has left by way of notes, and complete it during the course of the lesson, leaving it in the designated place as she leaves the classroom. The teacher can then check it at her leisure.

There is an unintended additional benefit to having the TA complete the log or pro forma during the lesson. While she is doing that, the student she supports is obliged to work independently, if only for a brief period. The student also becomes more aware that what he or she is doing and accomplishing during the lesson is being conveyed to the teacher.

- **Ask TAs to take notes on specific learning outcomes using the success criteria.**

  If you provide students with the learning outcomes for a lesson (by writing them on the board, for example), you can ask the TA to make comments in relation to the learning outcomes. Along with the outcomes you may well provide students with success criteria, so these too will help the TA provide specific and focused feedback that will help you in your subsequent planning for that class. To what extent did the student meet the success criteria? Which were most problematic? What did the TA do to help the student meet the criteria? And did it work? If the system you use in the school allows for it, the TA may be able to write notes on the IEP, which will support monitoring of pupil progress.

- **Ask the TA to carry out observations.**

  Periodically you might ask the TA to carry out an observation during part of the lesson, so that you have very specific formative data on which to base your future planning. This would be an observation of student learning and could focus on particular behaviours (on-task, responding to questions, collaborating with peers on an assigned task, for example) or she could more generally observe how a student spends their time during the 20 minutes or so of the observation. The target of the observation does not necessarily have to be a student allocated TA support – if observation data will help you to better meet the needs of more students, asking the TA to observe more generally will be a proper use of her time.

  The Welsh Assembly government produced a guidance document *Observing Children* in 2008 which you could use to help prepare your TA to conduct a systematic observation. This guidance can be downloaded for free from the Welsh government website (details in Appendix 1).

  If you are concerned about the lack of progress of a particular pupil it would be useful for the TA to carry out an observation on that child. For example, the TA might notice that when you tell the class to write something in their books that is when the pupil starts to misbehave. This information would help you to consider a strategy to avoid that happening; for example, to provide more support for him in writing by allowing the use of an iPad. This type of observation is a means of providing you with information in order to meet the needs of the pupil and thus improve performance.

What is an outstanding lesson?

The Ofsted framework does not say explicitly what an outstanding lesson should be, but it does provide an indication of what inspectors will look for in outstanding teaching. The key points that will set apart an outstanding lesson from one that is good or satisfactory are as follows:

- Work should be pitched at a level that is achievable if individual pupils work hard and try their very best.
- Assessment data should be used to set tasks that are perfectly matched to the pupils' prior attainment.
- The use of resources, *including the use of teaching assistants where applicable,* should promote rapid learning for pupils regardless of their aptitudes and needs.

(SecEd, 2012)

Suggest that the TA observe you as you teach a particular segment of a lesson, or use a particular teaching technique, so that she can learn from your expertise.

The previous suggestion related to observation of learning patterns – that is, observing student behaviours. Here we are suggesting that the TA observe teaching behaviours. This may take some courage on your part, as it can be unnerving to be observed by another adult. However, you need only do it when you are well prepared and ready to give something of a star performance. You may feel that it is not up to you to train the TA in this way, but if you want her to use particular, effective methods, you may need to be the one to draw her attention to them, and model best practice that she can follow. If she is to observe your teaching methods, it would be useful to have her make notes (for which we have provided a pro forma on page 113) and for you to get together with her at some point to discuss what she has observed. You can make it clear to her that this is not an evaluation, so she does not need to judge your performance or make any evaluative comment. She should just record what she sees or hears, objectively, and use it as a role model and then to reflect on her own practice.

- **Ask the TA for suggestions on how to enhance students' learning experience.**

The TA may accompany a student to a variety of lessons and may therefore have experience of a wide variety of strategies which have already been used with the student in other settings. She may also have worked with that student for a number of years. It would make sense therefore to ask her questions such as: *What seems to work for him/her in other settings/ classrooms?* Other useful questions that recognise the TA's knowledge of the student's strengths and needs might include:

- *I'm planning on doing [a particular sort of activity] this morning. Does he usually cope OK with that sort of thing?*
- *If we do some group work, does she generally do better just in a pair, or is she OK with a larger group?*
- *What types of situations/activities does he find particularly difficult/enjoyable?*
- *What do you usually do if... (e.g. the student can't manage the work or starts behaving badly)?*

These are of course the sort of questions you could ask the student in some cases, helping the student to become more aware of the strategies that have worked for him or her in the past, and the types of activities that they have enjoyed or found helpful.

- **Remember to convey to the TA her part in the management of behaviour in your classroom.**

    In the previous chapter we suggested that you clarify in your own mind what your preferences are for student behaviour, and then consider how you would like the TA to support your behaviour management regime. These are aspects that she will need to be clear about:

    - Be sure she knows what rewards and sanctions she can use to reinforce appropriate behaviour. (Is she allowed to give house points, or other tokens? What types of sanctions can she use?)
    - Make sure she knows you will support her if she has difficulties with a student who does not wish to comply with her requests. Statements to the student such as *If Mrs ... asks you to do something I expect you to do it please. She stands in for me when she's working with you. Please show her proper respect*, clearly display that you have confidence in the TA, and that the students will not able to ignore her requests without negative consequences.
    - Be open to questions from the TA during class time. When students are working independently the occasional *Everything OK?* directed at the TA shows her that you are available and willing to communicate during lesson time. If she asks a question that needs a longer response that might interrupt the current activity, agree to talk to her about it at a later time.
    - Make sure she knows whether she can write notes relating to behavioural targets or significant progress in the IEP/EHCP or on a sticky note so that you can transfer it onto the IEP/ECHP later. The actual writing down on a document/sticky note of the excellent behaviour of a student acts as an incentive for a continuation of that behaviour and subsequently the IEP/document can be used as an encouragement for good behaviour in the future e.g. *Remember last week I wrote down how well you...*

As a SENCO...

1. Consider whether you need to provide training for TAs on Assessment for Learning (AfL) and what they should and should not write in student books or on students' work.
2. Ensure that TAs understand that if they write on any document or piece of work they must include their initials and the date, as the comment may need to be traced back to the author for more information etc. for a review, for example.
3. If prompt aids, such as pictures or objects need to be made or collected, ensure that time is provided for that outside the lesson.
4. In order to collate information ready for IEP/EHCP annual reviews etc. time will be required. It may be that the school uses a person-centred approach to reviews so information gathering tools such as 'what's working/what's not working, good day bad day' will need to be obtained and time is needed for that.

Rob Webster, in his 2013 article 'A quiet revolution: How small changes to TA practice can yield big results', suggests five things that TAs can do to maximise their contribution to the classroom:

1. Know your role.
2. Hold your nerve.
3. Make what you say count.
4. Know what to do when you don't know what to do.
5. Extract the learning juice.

We have taken a look at his suggestions from a teacher or SENCO's point of view, to show how you can enable TAs to maximise their contribution in the ways he suggests. You can find our version in the nearby box, where you will also find the webpage for full details of what Rob Webster has suggested.

1. Know your role

Rob Webster points out that Teacher–TA liaison time before lessons is rare. This means that TAs don't necessarily know anything about the lesson they are about to attend – and in which they will have to provide support. This includes knowledge of content to be covered and tasks to be completed by the student, but also knowing what the teacher expects of them as the TA. Research has consistently shown that TAs tend to focus on 'getting the job done' – sometimes at the expense of real learning. They want to see a completed piece of work from the student – understandably, as it offers some sort of proof that they have been doing their job.

Two important statements come out of Rob Webster's article in this respect:

For the teacher: Good teachers *make the role they want TAs to take in lessons explicit,* and do not rely on TAs having to mind read.

For the TA: *Insist on knowing what the teacher expects from you at the start of the lesson* – and this includes specifics of the learning that is to take place, not just the tasks to be completed.

2. Hold your nerve

Here Rob Webster is referring to TAs' tendency to jump in too quickly to help students who are hesitant or lacking in confidence. As this increases a student's dependency on the TA, it is not helpful, especially in the long run. So you might usefully advise your TA:

- Please allow the student time to think for themselves – don't expect an answer straight away.
- Please *do not* provide the answer for the student to write down or copy, but encourage them to use strategies they have been taught to work out the answer on their own.
- Literally stand back from the student so that they can take more control of their own learning.

3. Make what you say count

Here the emphasis is on the fact that TAs have far more direct contact with students than you do as a teacher or SENCO, so that contact needs to be quality time. Suggestions here include training TAs to use more effective questions, as we have already suggested above.

4. Knowing what to do when you don't know what to do

TAs are often in the position of not actually knowing the answers to questions the student asks, because the TA cannot be an expert in every curriculum area. So a strategy suggested here – that you can pass on to your TA – is that they answer a question with another question. This again relates to developing students' independence by getting the student to draw on strategies he has already been taught – spelling rules, or using a dictionary, for example. Part of the TA's job is essentially to work herself out of her own job, because if a student can become an independent learner, the TA would no longer be needed. Throwing the ball back into the student's court is a strategy you can suggest to your TA, as a reminder that she really does not need to know all the answers, and the students need to be encouraged to think for themselves.

5. Extracting the learning juice

This is referring to the need for TAs to highlight successes for the supported student, and again link them to the strategies that enabled those successes. The student may not be willing to acknowledge the successes, as failing students generally have a very poor self-image. However, repeatedly flagging up the successful strategies will eventually convey the message: you are able to succeed, especially when you work smart. You can ask your TA to be sure to note these types of occurrences – for you and for the student.

Likewise the suggestion is made that TAs share moments of discouragement and 'failure' in their own learning and lives – times when they have not known the answers to questions, or not understood what was required of them. This helps the student to understand that others fail or falter too, and it is really just part of the learning process.

As Rob Webster states: "To sum up, if effective interactions are at the heart of good learning, as the research tells us it is, then improving how TAs interact with pupils could add serious value to the classroom."
     www.tafocus.co.uk/a-quiet-revolution-how-small-changes-to-ta-practice-can-yield-big-results/

Chapter summary

In this chapter we have been considering what you can do during lesson time to work more effectively with your TA. Following on from the pre-planning we discussed in the previous chapter, we have made the set of suggestions that can be seen in the box on the next page. These relate to involving the TA in all parts of the lesson, and your reversing the typical trend when there is a TA in the classroom, by working with a group of students yourself, and having the TA provide more general supervision for the rest of the class as they complete assigned tasks. We have also included a list of suggestions which you can give to a TA to remind her of how she can work more effectively with students. This can be copied and handed to your TA, or could be kept with other important information in a designated folder, if you are adopting that method for communication with your TA.

In a 2015 article in *Learning and Instruction*, researchers Radford, Bosanquet and Webster from the Institute of Education (IoE) and University of East London report findings from observation of TAs during maths and literacy lessons. They recommend differentiated roles for TAs according to individual student needs.

- *Support*, where TAs' main role would be to motivate and keep students on task.
- *Repair*, where TAs' main role would be to help students correct errors, but with an emphasis on supporting students as they evaluate and correct their own work, rather than doing this for them.
- *Heuristic*, which would involve TAs working with students to help them develop problem-solving strategies, thus empowering them as learners.

Ask yourself:

- Could this work in my setting? Would it be feasible to differentiate TA roles in this way (based on their experience and expertise)?
- What would we need to do to ensure that TAs fulfilled these roles appropriately, and thus meet the needs of individual students?

During the lesson: summary of suggestions

Involve TAs in all parts of the lesson

- Observe basic courtesies.
- Give the TA specific targets for their work, e.g. a certain group/individual/focus.
- Provide prompt sheets to support the TA's work with an individual student, e.g. questions they could ask pupils, differentiated outcomes.

Work with a group, e.g. not always the SEN/ targeted students

- Include TAs in the ongoing/formative assessment process during the lesson.
- Encourage TAs to feed back on learning outcomes and pupil responses to tasks.
- Ask TAs to take notes on specific learning outcomes using the success criteria.
- Ask the TA to carry out observations.
- Suggest that the TA observe you as you teach a particular segment of a lesson, or use a particular teaching technique, so that she can learn from your expertise.
- Ask the TA for suggestions on how to enhance students' learning experience.
- Remember to convey to the TA her part in the management of behaviour in your classroom.

Feedback sheet

Lesson	Date/ time
Teacher	Year group/students supported
Activity	

Comments
If appropriate comment on individual students' IEP targets

© 2016, *Achieving Outstanding Classroom Support in Your Secondary School*, J. Morgan, C. Jones and S. Booth-Coates, Routledge

General strategies for TAs during the lesson

Be clear about the needs of the individual pupil

Remember: It is not your role to do the work for them!!

These are some of the issues pupils may have in common:

- Low self-esteem
- Difficulty working independently
- Difficulty completing tasks
- Poor motivation

- Difficulty co-operating with peers
- Difficulty staying on task
- Poor communication skills

In the table you will find strategies for combatting these types of issues.

For pupils who have low self-esteem:	• Careful use of language • Genuine use of praise • Reward systems – personal, class, school • Ensure successful experiences – social and learning
For pupils who have difficulty cooperating with peers:	• Give them a position of responsibility • Make sure they are clear on the part they have to play • Make sure ground rules of their responsibilities are clearly laid out • Provide staged group work: ask them to cooperate with one other pupil, then with two pupils, then with a group of up to four selected pupils, to build their cooperative skills
To encourage independent working	Ensure: • clear organisation and labelling of resources • clear points of reference/timetables, etc. • a clearly spelled out routine that is adhered to • clear expectations of outcome • the student's contribution is valued by peers and adults • tasks are broken down into small, achievable chunks • the student is actively involved in the assigned task • key vocabulary is established and the student can recognise it in print • key vocabulary is used in written and oral instructions • reading is supported with symbols e.g write, draw, colour
To encourage staying on task	Ensure that there are: • reasonable and clear expectations • a distraction-free environment • verbal rehearsal of what is expected • self-monitoring of task completion • tangible markers for the passing of time e.g. using a timer • tasks of appropriate length for the time allocated • a marker to help keep the student's place in his/her work • appropriate rewards and sanctions which will not interfere unduly with completion of the work

© 2016, *Achieving Outstanding Classroom Support in Your Secondary School*, J. Morgan, C. Jones and S. Booth-Coates, Routledge

To encourage completion of tasks	Ensure: • the task is achievable • it is appropriate for the pupil • appropriate support is available • the student can carry out the actual processes involved • the student can concentrate for the required time • large tasks are broken into smaller chunks • the learning environment is conducive to completion • appropriate equipment is available • the pupil sits in a distraction-free position
If a child has poor communication skills	Ensure the pupil: • has the subject/area vocabulary needed • has the necessary grammatical skills • has the appropriate social vocabulary for the situation • can hear (no impairment) • utilises non-verbal cues as needed • is looking at the person talking • is in close proximity and has some eye contact
If a pupil has poor listening skills:	• Keep instructions simple – build up to complex multiple instructions • Use short phrases avoiding convoluted sentences • Establish a key/core vocabulary for a subject/area • Emphasise the key vocabulary of instruction • Repeat class instructions to a group or individual • Provide listening skills exercises • Provide opportunities to generalise skills learned
If a pupil has poor memory	Ensure the pupil has: • step-by-step short sequences • instructions given in point form • instructions given verbally • rote learning – a little at a time • learning with rhythm • verbal rehearsal – with/without prompts • interval recall – ask the pupil again after a period of time to ensure he/she has understood and knows what to do
Poor motivation	• Define the end-point – students are more likely to be motivated by tasks which they see as having a definite end-point than those which seem to stretch to infinity • Identify for the student that they can achieve the task – students will only be motivated by tasks they perceive as possible and within their capabilities • Be explicit about how the task is worthwhile and relevant to the student, citing both immediate (rewards, praise, sense of achievement) and long-term (how it will help them now, preparation for exams) benefits • Provide enjoyable and/or stimulating tasks • Avoid repeated failure – students with a long history of failure are unlikely to be motivated by a task they think there is a chance of failing again, so repeat practice exercises should, as much as possible, take a different format • Provide regular formative feedback – what has been done well, what still needs work • Reward, praise and support – regularly (not constantly) and genuinely • Develop positive relationships – students are more likely to attempt and persist in a task if they value their relationship with the adult who is working with them

© 2016, *Achieving Outstanding Classroom Support in Your Secondary School*, J. Morgan, C. Jones and S. Booth-Coates, Routledge

Bibliography

DCELLS (2008) *Observing Children*. Cardiff: WAG

Hattie, J. (2009) *Visible Learning: A Synthesis of Over 800 Meta-Analyses Relating to Achievement*. Abingdon: Routledge.

Neill, S.R.St.J. (2002) *Teaching Assistants:* A survey analysed for the National Union of Teachers. Warwick: University of Warwick Institute of Education, Teacher Research & Development Unit. Available at: www.leeds.ac.uk/educol/documents/151758.doc.

Radford, J., Bosanquet, P., Webster, R. and Blatchford, P. (2015) Scaffolding learning for independence: Clarifying teacher and teaching assistant roles for children with special educational needs. *Learning and Instruction* 36, 1–10.

SecEd (2012) *What Makes an Outstanding Ofsted Lesson*. Available at: www.sec-ed.co.uk/best-practice/what-makes-an-outstanding-ofsted-lesson (accessed 17.7.15).

Sharples, J., Webster, R. and Blatchford, P. (2015). *Making Best Use of Teaching Assistants*. London: Education Endowment Foundation.

Vincett, K., Cremin, H. and Thomas, G. (2005). *Teachers and Teaching Assistants Working Together: A Handbook*. Buckingham: Open University Press.

Webster, R. (2013) A quiet revolution: How small changes to TA practice can yield big results. Available at: www.tafocus.co.uk/a-quiet-revolution-how-small-changes-to-ta-practice-can-yield-big-results (accessed: 20.4.15).

Chapter 5

After the lesson

So you have delivered your lesson – approximately as planned. The class has left, and possibly the TA has left with them. What now? How does the TA feature in what you do as follow-up to lessons? You may have no time to take immediate action, but as you review your lesson later in the day or later in the week, this question will arise in relation to the TA and her contribution to the lesson.

To help answer this question it might be useful to start with what you normally do after a lesson. As classes come and go, you may only have time to draw breath or take a quick comfort break, but presumably at some point you engage in a review or reflect on each of the lessons you deliver in a day. This allows you to assess what was accomplished, and factor these accomplishments into the next lesson with that class. The important point here is to remember to include the TA's contribution in this general review exercise. We have included some questions that you might like to ask yourself about the TA's contribution on the next page, and as with the previous chapters, our suggestions follow.

Don't forget that crucial question: *What is it that I want from my TA?* As you review and evaluate your lessons, include consideration of what the TA was doing, and whether that represented what you would have liked to see her accomplish – not just in terms of the tasks completed, but in terms of her contribution to the teaching you had planned and the learning you hoped to see. Was she just child-minding? Or was she enhancing learning opportunities, for as many students as possible? And how do you know – were you able to monitor her work during the lesson?

After the lesson

1. Encourage feedback.
2. Show that you value your TA(s).

Encourage feedback

Good teaching depends on having good feedback. Good teachers are constantly responding to the feedback they receive from students, and making the necessary adjustments to their teaching as a result:

- You ask a question, and no one responds, so you re-phrase it.
- You ask a question and get incorrect answers so you re-visit the material, perhaps using additional illustrations or resources, and check again whether your students have understood.
- As you sense students' levels of engagement waning, you change activity to provide variety and inject new energy into the lesson.
- If students are particularly interested in one area of the current topic, you may allow discussions to go off at a tangent, because the enthusiasm and momentum are more important than just covering a set amount of material.

Post-lesson review: questions to ask about the TA's contribution to the lesson

- What was the TA doing for most of the lesson?
  - Helping a targeted student?

  - Sitting and listening to your delivery?

  - Helping other students?

  - Carrying out clerical /housekeeping tasks?

- What was the student supported by the TA doing for most of the lesson? (if applicable)

- What did the student supported by the TA accomplish during the lesson?
  - More or less than you had hoped?

  - More or less than the other students in the class?

- Could the TA's time have been put to better use?
  - How?

  - What would have been more helpful to you and the class in general?

© 2016, *Achieving Outstanding Classroom Support in Your Secondary School*, J. Morgan, C. Jones and S. Booth-Coates, Routledge

These are the sorts of decisions and adjustments you make every day, during every lesson, as a good teacher – all in response to the feedback you get from students. With the TA representing an extra pair of eyes and hands in the classroom, you can take advantage of her presence to increase the amount of informal data or feedback you gather about how students are behaving and responding to teaching. Here are some suggestions for how this might be accomplished.

- **Ask the TA to make brief notes about any issues during the lesson and pass them on.**

  As previously mentioned, a TA is well placed to provide feedback on the details of students' work and levels of understanding, particularly if she works with individuals or small groups. Your planning can include mechanisms for gathering this type of feedback from the TA, whether that be in person (outside the lesson period), or via sticky notes, log or feedback pro forma if meeting together is not feasible. This feedback should be couched in terms of the lesson objectives and students' individual targets if it is to be of maximum use to you in planning the next round of teaching. It also needs to be very specific. Comments such as *Yes, he did just fine,* are unhelpful. Ask the TA to refer to the lesson objectives and student targets and specify what the student accomplished in relation to each objective or target. This will help to produce more focused, formative feedback that will enable you to make evidence-based instructional decisions. Feedback may relate to behaviour or to elements of learning, including the student's response to questions, tasks set or activities.

  > Findings from the *Effective Deployment of TAs research* (Webster et al., 2013) showed that TAs were spending up to half of class time just listening while the teacher talked to the whole class – presenting new information or explaining what the students would be doing during the class period. This is obviously not good use of a TA's time (or of taxpayers' money!), although it is inevitable that a TA sometimes 'just' sit and listen to teacher talk, and necessary if she is to understand the material she will later help students with. You can make better use of this otherwise idle time if you ask the TA to carefully observe student reactions to your talk. Ask her to note:
  >
  > - Which students seem distracted or inattentive.
  > - If there is body language which suggests a student does not understand or is not following the instructions or grasping the new information.
  > - Any minor behavioural issues that you may not be able to see, but that she can from her different position in the class.
  >
  > Asking a TA to make these sorts of observations – and convey them to you using whichever method you have agreed between you beforehand – relays a clear message that she is needed, that she should be alert and contributing to the lesson even when she is not actively working with assigned students, and that her careful observations can help you to better meet the needs of all students.

- **This is a good reminder of the need to check: *Does the TA have email access? Does she have your email address and you hers?***

  Providing your work email to the TA is another signal that you want feedback – that you are open to her questions and would like her to communicate her observations to you. It allows her to convey information or address questions as they occur to her outside of class time and at her convenience, and of course you can respond when it is convenient for you. If your TA has not been provided with a work email address, you may prefer not to use a personal email. If this is the case, you might advocate for her (and the other TAs in the school) to have a school email address. You can make the suggestion to the SENCO who may be a member of the school leadership team, but will be able to pass your suggestion on for action.

- **Let the TA know when you are available for further discussion.**

As you may be aware, TAs often have other duties, such as lunch-time supervision, and are generally not paid to stay behind after school, unless they are running an after-school club – so you will need to be creative about finding time to get together to discuss lessons or students, or to engage in parts of the planning process together. You have assigned PPA time, so you could negotiate for the TA to occasionally come off timetable during your PPA time, so that you can discuss concerns or questions relating to students you both support. This does not have to take up all of your PPA time, nor does it have to occur every week – although regular discussions would obviously be helpful. The more this becomes part of your routine, the more efficient the process should become – you will be able to keep up to date through regular, brief discussions.

> TAs in primary schools may be assigned to provide cover for teacher PPA time; some TAs have this as a major or sole responsibility. Ironically some of them have no allocated PPA time themselves, despite having to plan and prepare lessons.
>
> Likewise when teachers have PPA time which is covered by their TA, this prevents the pair of them getting together to plan or prepare jointly.
>
> This is less likely to be the case in secondary schools, nevertheless it is a question that needs to be addressed: if we want our TAs to be better prepared, surely they need preparation and planning time. One aspect of that preparation and planning is to be able to plan and prepare with the teacher(s) to whose classes they are assigned. If you feel that this is important, you can advocate for it with the school leadership.

- **Consult the TA if you have to prepare information for reports or reviews.**

Your TA will probably know more about a student's general progress and achievements than you do if she works with the student in a variety of contexts and subject areas. She will also be able to supply more details of a student's attitudes and general understanding as she works closely with him/her in your classroom. So although you may have ready access to formal results and information such as the student's attendance, your TA should be able to supplement that information from her own experience of working with the student closely over a period of time. This richer level of detail is very valuable for giving a rounded picture of the student rather than just the bare facts. Knowing how the student copes in other subject areas also gives you insight into the student's strengths as well as his or her areas of need. You can draw on those strengths and may be able to incorporate them into your lessons, activities or approaches that have proven useful for the student in other curriculum areas.

Karen Littleton and Neil Mercer of Cambridge University talk about 'creative inter-thinking' and say that the brain is essentially a social organ, evolved to function within group settings (Littleton and Mercer, 2013). The marvellous thing about language, they say, is that it is a tool that allows us to think collectively, not just for transfer of information or ideas. Couple that with Vygotsky's theories of language influencing thinking, and thinking then influencing language, and you can see the increased potential for creative team working, as teachers and TAs (or SENCOs and TAs) get together to discuss what happens during lessons and explore how to improve and challenge students further. Verbalising ideas, or having to express thoughts or convey information requires us to organise those thoughts and ideas. Shared ideas can spark new thinking.

At the University of Queensland in Australia, Elizabeth Tatum has been investigating the usefulness of *Cogenerative Dialogue* for teachers and TAs who want to collaborate on their work (Ashbaker et al., 2015). Built on the idea of democratic dialogue, which involves turn-taking, active participation and collaborative discourse, *Cogenerative Dialogue* adds the elements of empowerment and equality. It offers possibilities for teachers (or SENCOs) and TAs to be proactive about making changes to their classroom practice, without waiting for changes in school policy or recommendations from official bodies (see Lehner, 2011 and Willis, 2013 in bibliography).

As a SENCO...

1. Depending on school policy and practice, it may be possible to invite the TA to review meetings (for IEPs /EHCPs, statements, etc.), although it would be advisable to brief her beforehand, to agree on what information she should and should not share in the meeting. A person-centred approach requires that anyone working with the student be present.
2. When you request information from the TA in preparation for such meetings, couch your request for information in terms of data and student targets. This will help to convey the importance of evidence, and make her contributions more specific and detailed. Be aware that the TA may need training to know how the review system works and how to share information appropriately.

Show that you value your TA(s)

As you consider how you can show appreciation for your TA, we could ask you to consider how *you* would like to have appreciation shown for your work, but instead we will ask you to think about: What makes you feel *un*appreciated? What do you grumble about *not* getting?

- Is it a general lack of consideration (of your time or preferences or convenience) when timetabling and other arrangements are made or changed?
- Is it that your opinions are neither sought, nor accepted when they are offered? That no one seems to value your advice or your prior and relevant experience?
- Is it that you feel ignored – in meetings, in the corridor – almost as if you don't exist for some people in the school? Perhaps that you are overlooked?
- Or it is that you feel your talents and strengths are not being put to good use – that there are ways in which you could contribute to the life of the school or to the plans for the department or faculty, but that no one seems to be interested in finding out that much about you?

Any one of these things can be very demoralising. A combination of them can really have a negative effect on your attitude to your work. So as you think of the things that make you feel *un*appreciated, convert that into actions – things you can do to show proper appreciation for the TA who works in your classroom, to prevent her feeling undervalued.

It is not necessary for everyone in a team to be equal, it is desirable that everyone should be equally valued.

(Collins and Lacey, 1996)

- **A thank you goes a long way!**

In the same way that a simple greeting when the TA enters your classroom takes little or no time, a simple *Thank you* as the TA leaves the room acknowledges the contribution she has made to the lesson, especially if you have had no opportunity during the lesson to exchange remarks. Hopefully she will think to return the courtesy, or thank you as she leaves. You may also want to consider whether a simple gift would be appropriate at Christmas time to express thanks for her ongoing support. In the back of the book you will find information on resources you could share with your TA. Some, like the books produced by Routledge and other publishers, are written specifically for TAs. Others, such as the Teachers TV clips (now available through YouTube) are for a more general audience, but may not be known to your TA. There are also many items specifically for TAs on the YouTube website.

- **Acknowledge TAs outside the classroom environment.**

Again, a simple greeting when you pass the TA elsewhere in the school acknowledges their presence and contributions. It is also important that you back her up if she is dealing with difficult students around the school. Although the majority of TAs may be well respected by students and staff alike, TAs and students tell us that there can still be an attitude of '*You're just a TA – I don't have to do what you tell me.*' This is particularly likely in situations where the TA is the only adult, such as in the corridors or at break and lunch time. So you may come across a situation where students are refusing to do what a TA has quite legitimately asked them to do – in accordance with the school rules. It can be a tricky situation to handle, because you do not want to just take over and have the students do as *you* tell them – you want to reinforce the TA's authority and send a clear message that they are to do as she asks, particularly when it is in line with the school rules or policy. So you may need to think this through.

> We asked secondary school students how they thought TAs were generally viewed by students. They said:
>
> - *Not respected, for example if a TA told a student off they would be like 'You can't tell me off, you're not a teacher.'*
> - *People don't take them that seriously.*

If you were the TA, what would you want a teacher to say that would back you up rather than just substituting for you? What would you *not* want the teacher to say? How would you *not* want the teacher to handle this? Remember the desired outcome of this interaction with the students is that the TA's authority is clearly established and confirmed. You might want to consider phrases such as:

> *Well Mrs T, do we have a little problem here?* (The 'we' indicating that you and she are together in this)

You might also wish to talk to the TA later about how best to handle such situations. Let her know that you are happy to support her, and that you want to reinforce her authority, not undermine it. She may not feel confident that the students will do as she asks, and you may have felt that way yourself, especially as a new teacher. Keeping calm and adopting a reasonable tone is always a good approach. So encourage her to be firm, to re-iterate the rule the students are not complying with, and to use the phrase '*You need to ...*' rather than asking them to change their behaviour: *Are you going to do as I ask or not?* This type of question invites the answer *No,* and offers the option of defiance, which could make the situation worse.

If she is having this type of difficulty and wants a passing member of staff to support her, suggest some ways she could phrase her difficulties in front of the students without sounding as if she is asking to be rescued.

- **If you see inappropriate behaviour or interactions from a TA, express your concerns to the SENCO and request training.**

It makes sense to let the SENCO (or other TA line manager) know if you have concerns about a TA, and advocate for training for her. This is the same sort of formative feedback loop you use in your teaching – you spot an error or lack of understanding on the part of a student, and intervene to correct that error or misunderstanding so that it is not perpetuated, and the student can move on in the right direction. Most TAs will be grateful for opportunities to learn and improve, and although they may be embarrassed by the idea that someone has noticed them doing something badly, that negative feeling should be counterbalanced by the training they receive to improve their knowledge and practice. And of course a diplomatic and practical SENCO would offer training to a group of TAs, rather than singling out one.

A 2010 report into the implementation of the *National Agreement* in Wales (DCELLS, 2010) cited examples seen of good practice in relation to upskilling staff. These included:

ensuring appropriate professional development opportunities, enabling support staff to develop interests and expertise, delivering in-service training on a whole-school basis, offering joint training to TAs and NQTs, encouraging support staff to develop knowledge of the pupils and their background, and strengthening systems to share information between teachers and support staff.

- **Invite your TAs to social events.**

If staff are getting together socially, for example on a departmental basis, consider inviting the TAs who work in the department as a mark of their inclusion in the instructional team.

The TA may choose not to attend, but it is the fact of being invited that often matters most. That is the mark of consideration, the signal that she is part of the team. Likewise if you have traditions in your school (the birthday girl/boy gets to buy cakes for the whole department, for example) include your TA in that arrangement. If the cakes bought by the teachers do not make it to where the TA spends their break times, you can change that, or at least send something out to the TA in the playground.

- **Raise the issue of TAs at meetings to which they are not invited.**

There may be staff or faculty meetings to which TAs are not invited, but where topics discussed would be of interest and relevance to TAs. In fact, realistically there are very few issues that would not be of relevance to TAs as members of the instructional team. These may relate to school policy, timetabling arrangements, new initiatives or even training opportunities, and this is another way in which you can advocate for your TA. Don't forget to ask, at the meeting:

- Will the TAs be included in this initiative/project/training?
- How will the TAs get this information?
- Can I take a copy of this for my TA?

If you have an active SENCO in your school, the information would normally be passed on to the TA as a matter of course, and some schools have designated senior TAs or TA managers, but they may not be invited to all staff meetings. The fact that you are asking these questions will raise awareness of the need to include TAs in the whole life of the school, and make it more likely that appropriate information is passed along. And everyone expects the SENCO to take care of the TAs, so the fact that a classroom teacher is asking these questions will hopefully alert other teachers to the idea that they also come under the teacher's remit.

What this will do in addition is wave the flag for TAs so they are not overlooked. It will remind senior management, or whoever is running the meeting, that TAs are part of the team, and need to be kept informed of important school developments. And of course the TAs are then also better equipped to support the initiatives or projects that the school is undertaking.

This is especially important when the discussion relates to behaviour. When there are changes of policy or practice in relation to behaviour, the TA needs to know. If a TA is seen to be ill-informed about changes in policy or procedure, it undermines her authority with students. It is very disconcerting to be ill-informed, and as TAs often have other duties during break or lunchtimes, and generally cannot stay behind for after-school meetings, it is easy for them to miss information and get left out of the communication loop. This also seriously compromises the consistency which is so essential to a whole-school approach to behaviour.

As a SENCO...

Training

1. Provide ongoing training for TAs especially in behaviour management. This is particularly important to ensure consistency of approach and response to both appropriate and inappropriate behaviour. TAs may encounter quite a wide variety of styles of behaviour management if they attend a number of different classrooms. However, the basic principles should be consistent across the school. TAs should know how to access the school behaviour policy, or a copy should be provided for them. They need to know what rewards and sanctions are available to students, and which of these they are authorised to provide.

2. While TAs may not be used to reading research articles or more formal academic writing, there are plenty of teaching resources available that you no doubt access yourself, and that you could share with the TA. For example, nasen produces *The British Journal of Special Education* and *Support for Learning*, which are both academic publications, but it also produces *Special* which has a more practical, everyday focus, and includes articles on specific special or additional learning and support needs, and on more general topics such as behaviour, literacy, etc. If you – or the school – have a subscription to such publications, and you see an article that you think would be relevant, why not flag it up to the TAs, or make photocopies for them. If you are keeping a folder in your room for communications with TAs, you could slip the article in there so that they see it when they next come into the room. If the school subscribes

to a subject-specific publication (such as *Teaching English* or *Mathematics Teaching*), all the better if you can give the TA access to articles that relate directly to the subject matter for the classes in which she provides support. We have also included a list of books for TAs in Appendix 2.

Creative use of TAs' time

A common complaint when school staff are confronted with the need to collaborate (with TAs or other members of staff) is that there just is not enough time in the school day for everything that is already required of them, so how can they possibly find even more time for working or planning with TAs, or for providing training. As we have already noted, this all generally needs to take place during the school day as most TAs' contracts do not extend beyond, either before or after school. A variety of approaches have been used by schools to tackle this issue:

- TAs stay behind for 30 minutes once a week for planning meetings with teaching staff. Once per half-term they are given a half-day off in lieu (usually a Friday afternoon, as this is a time when lessons are less structured and many students can manage without support), avoiding the controversial issue of additional payment.
- TAs have regular meetings with the SENCO during school assemblies, unless they are assigned to a student who needs support during that type of activity.
- TAs are timetabled for preparation and planning (in the same way that teachers are allocated PPA time) as part of their contracted hours, and in recognition of the fact that they may need time to prepare resources, to record student accomplishments or difficulties, or to follow up on an issue that has arisen during the week.

A 2005–6 inspection survey in Northern Ireland (Education and Training Inspectorate (N. Ireland), 2005–6) reported that the majority of Classroom Assistants (CAs) who worked with students with special needs would value opportunities for additional training, whether it led to an accredited qualification or not. They were particularly interested in training relating to their daily work and that had direct practical application. A small number of the CAs reported that they had attended – in their own time and at their own cost – conferences and workshops organised by local SEN interest groups. Their main aim was to further their own knowledge of the needs of the students they supported.

The 2005–6 inspectorate report also noted improvements in understanding and management of CAs in schools where those CAs had been encouraged to attend training and take advantage of advice available to them.

Employment and deployment

You may be familiar with the SENCO forum which is regularly reported in the *British Journal of Special Education* (BJSE). If not, we would recommend that you join with other SENCOs across the UK in the online discussions that are reported. In a 2011 discussion, the following issues were raised in relation to TAs.

1. Whether TAs should be allocated by department or to individual students. The dilemma is whether it is better to use a TA's knowledge of the student or knowledge of a curriculum area. This depends partly on the needs of the student – for example, for a student with visual impairment (VI), knowledge of the student's needs would be imperative, whatever the subject area; giving the student support from a variety of subject-expert TAs as he/she moves from one

lesson to another is not likely to represent the best support because of the particular needs associated with VI. However, as subject knowledge is so critical at secondary level, having the TA as a second subject 'expert' could provide better levels of support for students whose needs are less specialised than a physical disability such as VI.

> The 2015 Ofsted school inspection handbook states that there will now be a focus on *ensuring teaching assistants are knowledgeable about pupils they support and have sufficient subject knowledge to be effective in their role.*

2. Whether the school allocates time for the TA and teacher to plan together. This is easier if the TA is department based – and the question was asked whether the SENCO could offer to cover a lesson to enable this – although it would be difficult for the SENCO to cover for more than a small number of teachers so that they can plan with their TA(s).
3. How carefully TAs are selected for employment in the first place, and the extent to which their knowledge and skills are taken into account in the selection process. This no doubt occurs in a general sense – the candidates with better qualifications and greater experience are more likely to be successful – but the issue is whether this is linked to the specific support needs in the school at the time of hiring.

> There was a need to ensure that teachers, particularly new entrants, were trained about how to work with support staff to best effect. There was also a need to enable support staff and teachers to plan together and for classroom-based support staff to be given their own planning and preparation time where appropriate (DCELLS, 2010).

Valuing TAs

Below you will find a case study *In Praise of Mrs P.* which provides a slightly different perspective on TAs and the support they can offer.

We can learn from Mrs P. (who is a real person) and use her strategies to improve the lot of students who are struggling. Notice how proactive Mrs P. was – she negotiated, she offered a solution to a problem, she approached teachers. How does a TA gain that much confidence to be that proactive on behalf of students? As we show how much we value TAs – their contributions to the classroom and to student learning, their ideas and suggestions – perhaps we will see more of the sort of initiative shown by Mrs P. People who feel valued also feel more confident, and more able to contribute. The majority of TAs are very competent individuals who run homes and raise families, who may even run charities and marathons in their spare time. We need to recognise them as such, tap into their current skills and knowledge, and do what we can to enhance their effectiveness.

Case study: in praise of Mrs P.

Jane was diagnosed with autism during her primary school years. Those were very difficult years and Jane's mother, Karen, struggled with the decision whether to take her out of school entirely or allow her to transition into secondary education. With some misgivings, she decided in favour of the secondary school, which bordered on the primary school where Karen worked.

At break- and lunchtime, Karen would see her daughter out on the perimeter fence on her own, and would go out and talk to her. Jane didn't mix well with other children, and was more at ease on her own, but Karen hated to see her there alone. One breaktime they were approached by a woman who introduced herself as Mrs P. – a Teaching Assistant in the secondary school. She too had noticed Jane out by the fence every breaktime, had noticed her talking to Karen, and had come to see if she could help in any way. She was already assigned to support Jane in English lessons – although Jane really didn't seem to need her support – but had heard that Jane was experiencing difficulties in other curriculum areas. Mrs P. promised Karen that she would see if she could do anything to help Jane in those lessons. Karen was pleased that someone was taking an interest in Jane, but not especially optimistic – after all, they'd experienced years of difficulties despite a succession of well-meaning teachers and TAs in the primary school. But this is some of what Mrs P. did:

- Negotiated her timetable so that she wasn't supporting Jane in English, where she really wasn't needed.
- Asked to be timetabled instead to another curriculum area in which Jane had insufficient support and was struggling – as Jane already knew Mrs P. she would not have to deal with the social issue of getting to know a new TA.
- Spoke to each of the teachers who taught Jane, to let them know about Jane's strengths and needs, so that they were better prepared to include her in the lessons, offering suggestions for ways in which they could modify their practice to better accommodate Jane.

Life didn't magically become easy for Jane or her teachers, but it did improve significantly, and she left secondary school with a set of qualifications that surpassed those of many of her peers, and to everyone's delight she was able to go on to study at university.

From across the Atlantic

The IDEA Partnership Paraprofessional Initiative, reporting to the US Department of Education (USDE, 2001) identified supervision needs at various levels in and aspects of the education system. This included:

1. That the school leadership need to clearly distinguish between the roles and responsibilities of teachers/SENCOs and TAs; assigning appropriate roles so that staffing patterns meet individual student needs.
2. Making 'supervisor of TAs' a distinct role and assignment – whether this be the SENCO, a TA manager, or head of faculty/department. If TAs are allocated thus, time should be allocated to facilitate the role.
3. Training for those who supervise TAs.
4. Time allocated for TAs to plan, gather appropriate equipment and resources (and set up the learning environment where they are assigned, if needed).
5. Families need to understand who is directing and monitoring the performance of TAs.

This list shows how comprehensively schools need to plan for effective deployment of TA, and highlights the extent of the infrastructure required to ensure that TAs receive the supervision they need in order to work effectively within their assigned roles.

Chapter summary

In this chapter we have been looking at actions that teachers and SENCOs might take after a lesson is completed. This may not be immediately after, but is likely to result from a review of the lessons where a TA has been present. We have presented these actions in terms of *Encouraging feedback* from the TA, and *Showing that you value the TA,* although both of these relate to valuing the TA's contributions. The research consistently shows that TAs feel more valued when they are included and consulted – as you no doubt feel more valued when you are included or consulted on matters of importance. And feedback is essential for effective teaching, so it is a matter of prime importance. Consulting a TA and asking for feedback acknowledges that, although she may not have the same level of qualifications that you have, she most likely does have experience to draw on. And even the most inexperienced TA will have an opinion that can be considered, and will be able to provide useful information relating to student needs and progress. We have made several suggestions here for upskilling TAs, whether through formalised training or through informal but regular discussions with teachers. This, coupled with the observations we suggested in the last chapter, can bring a much more professional approach to a TA's work, and convey the message that inclusive schools include all adults, not simply all students in the teaching and learning process.

After the lesson: summary of suggestions

1. Encourage feedback.
    *   Ask the TA to make brief notes about any issues during the lesson and pass them on.
    *   This is a good reminder of the need to check: Does the TA have email access? Does she have your email address and you hers?
    *   Let the TA know when you're available for further discussion.
    *   Consult the TA if you have to prepare information for reports or reviews.
2. Show that you value your TAs.
    *   A thank you goes a long way!
    *   Acknowledge TAs outside the classroom environment.
    *   If you see inappropriate behaviour or interactions from a TA, express your concerns to the SENCO and request training.
    *   Invite your TAs to social events.
    *   Raise the issue of TAs at meetings where they are not included.

Bibliography

Ashbaker, B.Y., Tatum, E. and Morgan, J. (2015) Sharing and learning from paraeducators around the world. Paper presented at the 32nd Annual Conference of the National Resource Center for Paraprofessionals. Hartford, Connecticut.

Collins, M. and Lacey, P. (1996) *Interactive Approaches to Teaching.* London: David Fulton.

DCELLS (2010) *Research into the National Agreement on Raising Standards and Tackling Workloads.* Cardiff: WAG.

Education and Training Inspectorate (N. Ireland) (2005–6) *Effective Use of Assistants for Pupils with Special Educational Needs in Mainstream Schools.* Report of an Inspection survey. Belfast: ETI (NI).

Estyn (2011) *Guidance for the Inspection of Secondary Schools.* Cardiff: Estyn.

Lehner. E. (2011) Employing cogenerative dialogue to share classroom authority. *Education Research Journal* 1 (6), pp. 94–104. Available at: resjournals.com/ERJ/Pdf/Nov/Ed%20Lehner.pdf.

Littleton, K. and Mercer, N. (2013) *Interthinking: Putting Talk to Work.* Abingdon: Routledge.

Ofsted (2015). *The Framework for School Inspection.* London: Ofsted.

US Department of Education (2001) *The IDEA Partnership Paraprofessional Initiative*. Report to the USDE (OSEP). Washington, DC: USDE.

Webster, R., Blatchford, P. and Russell, A. (2013) Challenging and changing how schools use teaching assistants: findings from the Effective Deployment of Teaching Assistants project. *School Leadership & Management* (Formerly School Organisation), 33 (1), pp. 78–96. Also available at: http://maximisingtas. co.uk/assets/content/edta-project-final.pdf.

Willis, L.-D. (2013) Parent-teacher engagement: a coteaching and cogenerative dialoguing approach. Unpublished doctoral dissertation, Queensland University of Technology, Australia. Available at: eprints. qut.edu.au/63306/1/Linda-Dianne_Willis_Thesis.pdf.

Conclusions

An overview

In the first part of this book, we looked at the background to the employment of TAs in schools and the now extensive research relating to effective deployment of TAs, with particular reference to secondary school settings and mainstream education. Although many TAs were originally employed to work with students with special or additional learning needs, large numbers also now work providing more general support in schools with high levels of students whose first language is not English, or schools in deprived areas, as the impact of socio-economic factors has been recognised as a potential barrier to learning. Such is the reliance on Teaching Assistant support that the total number of TAs in schools in England exceeds the number of teachers employed in those schools.

Recent research has highlighted some of the pitfalls of this reliance on support staff – who largely have only limited formal qualifications, but whose roles are often varied but specialised. They may be assigned to support students with a variety of different needs; they are also often assigned to students with very particular difficulties. This is of special concern in secondary settings where there is the added complication of TAs supporting students in curriculum areas in which they (the TAs) may have only limited content knowledge. The other major concern identified by current research is the extent of student dependence on TAs – and therefore their lack of developing independent study and self-help skills. These are not new concerns, as they have been highlighted in the professional and academic literature for many years now. However, in the current evidence-based education culture, we now have firm evidence of the impact of TAs' work and can target the identified areas of shortfall for training. There are larger systemic issues to be addressed by school leadership and institutions of higher education which provide initial teacher education programmes. But the purpose of this book is to provide teachers and SENCOs with greater awareness of the issues and practical suggestions for changes they can make to their own practice in their own sphere of influence, all the while advocating for the changes in the system such as joint planning time for teachers and TAs, and better preparation for TAs for the roles they are assigned.

In the first section of the book we also included a section on differentiation or personalisation of learning, because the majority of TAs are employed in order to support inclusion, which requires differentiation of tasks, approaches and support to allow all students access to the curriculum and maximised opportunities for learning. But as we noted in Chapter 2, the evidence suggests that many TAs have become an alternative rather than a supplementary provision, so their work may actually be fostering segregation for supported students.

- Segregation from their peers because they are too often assigned to work one-to-one with a TA; this can produce both an instructional and a social segregation.
- Segregation from the teacher, as they (and their provision) are entrusted largely to a TA, so contact with the teacher may be minimal; inadvertently teachers can allow this to happen as

they see their responsibility as being for the whole class and are relieved and reassured that the student who finds the work most challenging has individual support from the TA.

- Segregation from the highest quality instruction because the student's work is not being overseen and managed by the teacher – the expert in both curriculum and pedagogy – but by a TA, who may not have received training in either subject matter or teaching strategies.

As we have already highlighted, the 2015 SEND Code of Practice in England clearly states that teachers are responsible for the progress of all students, including those with special or additional learning needs. This has always been true, but the 2015 legislation states it boldly and clearly. TAs are to support learning and teaching, for which the teacher has overall responsibility.

Those who have conducted recent research into the deployment of TAs and the impact of their work have concluded that this is a leadership issue. Whatever shortcoming the research may have revealed in TAs' work, if blame is to be assigned, it should certainly not fall on TAs, who are working as assigned and do not often contribute to decisions about their work patterns or specific assignments. Decisions about their deployment are made by the school leadership or management team. Likewise, the attitude of the school leadership towards TAs and the contribution they make to learning largely determines the attitude taken across the school, so if the whole-school approach to use of TAs is to change, that must come from those who have leadership responsibilities. And lastly, the extent of the professional development opportunities offered to TAs is also largely determined by school leadership, as few TAs are in a position to pursue their own professional development on their own time or finances.

Throughout the book we have been asking the crucial question: *What is it that you want from your TA?* Not in terms of tasks set and completed, but in terms of the contribution she makes to the core work of the school: high-quality teaching and success for students. Again, this really is a leadership issue, but it is also a question that teachers and SENCOs should be asking themselves, as they work most closely with TAs on a day-to-day basis. As we hope you have found through reading the book, there are many ways in which you can enhance the effectiveness of your work with TAs – which in turn enhances the contribution that she can make to the work of the school. Let's review some of the ideas that we have presented for your consideration.

In Chapter 3 we looked at how TAs should feature in a teacher's planning *before* lessons are taught – that as a teacher plans the resources for lessons, the TA's presence, skills and experience should be included as one of the resources available. We urged teachers to be flexible in using the TA – to allow the TA to supervise independent tasks assigned to a class while the teacher works with a group of struggling students, for example; to have the TA collect data, or observe the teacher to see examples of good practice and in turn improve her own practice. These examples of good practice must be planned for. They will not happen in the course of a busy day of teaching unless they are carefully considered beforehand, and embedded into a teacher's normal way of working.

We also made some suggestions for how SENCOs can contribute to this forward planning for more effective working with TAs. This really is a point at which a SENCO can influence effectiveness, as they carefully consider assignments and support needs alongside TAs' skills and knowledge. What needs to be done? And who is the best person to do it from among those available to you? If you really do not have someone amongst the TAs who is skilled enough, what can be done to upskill someone? And who would be the most appropriate person? Is this something that you can do yourself? Or will you need support from an external agency, such as the local authority?

In Chapter 4 we considered ways in which the TA can be incorporated into the delivery of the lesson, especially in relation to providing feedback to both the students and the teacher or SENCO. Again, we emphasised the importance of flexibility of working. The 2015 SEND Code of Practice in England allows for this type of flexibility, even when individual students are allocated a specified number of hours of support each week. That support can take a whole variety of forms and should not solely consist of TA time. Parents can be reassured that their child is receiving the best type of support, and at the prescribed level, but in a variety of formats (group work to help develop collaborative skills, supported by the teacher on occasions, or the TA, individual tasks to help develop independence, etc.).

For SENCOs we emphasised the need to consider training for TAs, in line with the current support needs of the school. There are certain areas in which all TAs could benefit from training – the use of Assessment for Learning (if that is an approach adopted by the whole school), the collection of data to assist teachers in making databased decisions and contribute to reports and reviews. We also highlighted the need to be flexible in assigning support staff.

In Chapter 5 we considered some of the ways teachers can continue to work 'with' and for the TA even after a lesson, by advocating for greater inclusion of TAs in the organisational meetings and teams of the school, facilitating training opportunities for the TA, and showing support for the TA in front of students, particularly if students are not showing an acceptable level of respect for the TA and her authority while on the school premises. For SENCOs we suggested inviting TAs to review meetings, provided they have been briefed beforehand as to protocol and the type of information they should share with the team. We again referred to the need for training, particularly in behaviour management, to ensure the consistency that is essential for a whole-school approach. But we also recommended sharing resources with TAs, so that they can engage in constant upgrading of their knowledge and skills. A SENCO really is in the best position to advocate for TAs (particularly if the SENCO is part of the school leadership team), and to negotiate the type of arrangements which allow for planning time for TAs, time for TAs and teachers to occasionally but regularly meet together, and off-site professional development specific to the role of the TA. We also raised the issue of performance monitoring or appraisals for TAs. This may be assigned to the SENCO as the TA's line manager, or may be taken on by a member of the school leadership team. If the TA's work is not currently being appraised, the SENCO could advocate for that to be initiated; however, it should be based on the TA's assigned roles, rather than being based on more general teacher responsibilities and appraisal.

You may be interested to know that a checklist for TAs can be found on the nasen website. In chart format it suggests elements that a TA should attend to under the headings 'Before the lesson starts', 'During the lesson introduction', 'During whole-class work', 'In group work', 'In plenary sessions', 'At the end of the lesson' and 'After the lesson'. It is Activity Sheet 4 of the *Working with Others* module: *Monitoring the Role of Additional Support in the Classroom,* and can be photocopied for your TAs. Details of the nasen online training materials can be found in Appendix 1.

In each of these chapters we have also made suggestions for how the SENCO can also support a change of practice and approach with regard to how TAs are deployed and generally valued and included in the instructional team. SENCOs are sometimes designated members of the school leadership team and are thus more able to influence decisions made about TAs and their work. But even SENCOs who are not considered part of the leadership of the school can advocate for TAs, and for the TA–teacher teams which operate in the school, as they have a better overview of the issues and the responsibilities than most other members of staff.

Themes that have emerged

In the remainder of this chapter we draw together some of the themes that have emerged throughout the book:

- The need to plan for planning.
- Building in feedback mechanisms.

- The importance of developing a working relationship with the TA.
- Ways in which the TA's status and profile can be raised, engendering greater respect among staff and students, etc.

Planning for planning. The importance of planning for effective teaching was clearly highlighted by the *National Agreement* which required that teachers be allocated designated Preparation, Planning and Assessment (PPA) time. This remains a basic entitlement of teachers under the terms and conditions of their employment. Logically, if the teacher is to plan for the TA's work as one of the supports for differentiation, including the TA in the planning would also make sense.

Building in feedback mechanisms. Assessment was also recognised through the *National Agreement* as a crucial element of quality teaching. It would be foolish to have at one's command a source of assessment information and not make full use of it. As we have already discussed at some length here, TAs are potentially a highly valuable source of formative assessment data which teachers can feed into their planning to ensure that they are meeting the needs of all students by building on what the students know and can do.

Developing a working relationship with the TA. Good working relationship are built on mutual respect and trust. A teacher should be able to entrust delivery of parts of the teaching process to a TA, knowing that the TA has the necessary skills and knowledge to carry out that role competently. That suggests the need for teachers knowing what the TA's capabilities are, and assigning tasks that are suitable, given those capabilities. Likewise a TA should be able to trust the teacher to have due concern for her needs and interests as well as those of the students. So the TA should have confidence that the teacher will not require more of her than is reasonable, and that he or she will back her up in front of students if necessary and appreciate the contributions the TA makes, whether that be suggestions for improvement, feedback on students' work, or questions about practice.

Raising the profile and status of TAs. This is not a question of raising the profile of TAs nationally or publicly. This is largely a question of raising the profile of TAs within the school, for all staff, including the senior management team. Raising awareness of the contribution that TAs currently make, the contribution which the school needs them to make, and the possible gap between those two markers. What is needed to fill that gap? We talk of closing the gap for students – meaning the achievement gap – not just in terms of a student being behind his or her peers, but also the gap between what the student currently achieves and what he or she could achieve. Many students who are supported by TAs are under-achieving students, not students who are incapable of achieving. Likewise, we need to close the achievement gap for TAs – the gap between what they now achieve and what we believe they could achieve, given the necessary support. Like our under-achieving students, many TAs are under-achieving because they have not had what they need to succeed. And given the major contribution they are expected to make to our schools, they too need an accelerated programme of learning.

Under all these headings we would suggest that both teachers and SENCOs have a certain autonomy. Although the precise details of the deployment of TAs is a school-wide and leadership issue, teachers and SENCOs can take the lead and make changes to their own practice *even when there seems to be little institutional enthusiasm or drive for it.* You can be a leader even if you are not in a leadership position in the school, by taking the initiative and changing some of the ways you have worked in the past, to include the TA in your instructional planning and practice.

Jenny Versey, an education consultant and a former school improvement adviser, offers a self-evaluation for science teachers who work with TAs. We feel that the questions she asks are relevant to any subject areas, so we have included them in Table 6.1. They represent a simple audit of the

TA's work. A much more comprehensive, school-wide audit of the deployment of TAs is provided in Anne Watkinson's (2008) book *Leading and Managing Teaching Assistants,* where she devotes a whole chapter to consideration of the variety of ways this can be accomplished, with real-life examples from schools. A school-wide audit has been developed by the authors of the *Maximising the Impact of TAs* research. We have not included it here as you can download it for free from the MITA website (listed in Appendix 1). There you will find both a staff survey and an observation pro forma, together with detailed guidance on how to conduct the audit. This will help to provide baseline data and identify areas for change and improvement.

Jenny Versey highlights the importance of monitoring how TAs are deployed and regularly reflecting on whether the best use is being made of their time. She offers the following points for consideration, with suggestions for change, which we have further developed in Table 6.1.

We also recognise that you will not be dealing with just one TA in your classroom. As a secondary school teacher, the greater likelihood is that you will have a number of TAs in the room with you over the course of a typical week. And yes, this does mean that you need to consider the points we have made for each of those TAs in order to have the most effective support for all your students. But start smart. Start with the TA you feel you will best be able to work with. You do not need to start with the TA who you think will be reluctant to engage with you or change her ways. Hone your skills on the willing before you take up that challenge! We know that TAs are no different from any other group of people, in that you will find amongst them those who can and will cooperate, change and adapt – and those who will not; those who want to learn and improve their own effectiveness – and those who do not.

Table 6.1 The work of TAs: questions and suggestions

Question	Suggestion
1. For how much of the lesson time is the TA passively listening to the teacher along with students?	Aim to keep this to a minimum (or as we have suggested in a previous chapter, assign the TA to observe and report her observations as she listens)
2. With how many students does the TA interact?	Aim to maximise this number (as we have suggested by permitting the TA to rove, or by assigning her to a group rather than an individual)
3. Does the TA regularly scan the students for off-task behaviour?	They should be proactive in doing this as another adult in the room
4. Have you ever asked your TA for advice?	Do so – they can often provide a different perspective, even seeing things through the student's eyes, and make suggestions for improvement
5. Have the TAs who support [curriculum area] received any training in [curriculum area]?	Jenny Versey is providing this advice to Science teachers and suggests that there are ample training opportunities through Science education entities. We would suggest that subject teachers in the school could provide TAs with training in their own subject content

Adapted from: Versey (2006).

There are of course those who say that if you can get something to work with the most difficult or resistant group of students, it will work for anyone. But we would not push you into tackling the most resistant TAs unless you really feel the need for a new challenge!

Making the investment

The types of activity we have recommended throughout this book must really be seen as an investment – of time and effort – in order to achieve a desired outcome. First, because the desired change is not likely to happen instantly – the small contributions you make to your savings plan or investment portfolio may seem pitiful to begin with, but saving is a long-term activity and you can expect to see growth over time. Investing in TAs will take some time and effort on your part – but will hopefully be rewarded by seeing a willing TA extend her usefulness and skills. Investing time and effort in this way is not only an investment in TAs but, by extension, an investment in improved student engagement, retention and performance.

The other way in which this is an investment is because to some extent it will take you away from your teaching duties – not for long periods of time, but consistently over time – so that, through your supervision, the TA will be a more effective support. Committing yourself to a savings plan or investment portfolio does usually mean that you have to be willing to give up a little of something else that you could have spent the money on. So, with your TA, you expend some time and effort, and give up some of the precious time available for teaching so that in the long run you can lead a more effective classroom team. You can be efficient and effective as a teacher for most of your students on your own. But TAs are assigned to some of your most difficult students so that you can be efficient and effective for those students too – and that means bringing the TA into your teaching, and working *with* her, so that you can both be more effective for all of your students. This is one of the realities of modern classroom life – adults working together for student success. It may not have been the job you signed up for; it may not have been part of your initial training or figured in subsequent in-service or professional development. However, it clearly is now one of your responsibilities as the professional in the classroom.

Do the maths

Five minutes of your time out of a lesson – but not necessarily every lesson – is only 5 minutes of teaching time lost. But if those 5-minute interactions with your TA make her twice as effective in helping the student to build confidence, knowledge and understanding, and in supporting your teaching, then it is worth the investment. And the 5 minutes accumulate to constitute a regular professional development for the TA. Over the course of a school year, even 5 minutes per week spent with you focusing on some aspect of her professional development will amount to the TA receiving several hours of training. Those minutes also show your levels of commitment and professionalism, your willingness to show leadership and work collaboratively. All as stated in the teacher standards, and as expected by the school inspectorate. All in all, surely it's worth 5 minutes of your time here and there.

James Richardson in a blog on 9 March 2015 (www.nahtedge.org.uk) said:

> The overarching message for teachers, and particularly those in middle leadership positions with the responsibility for deploying TAs, is positive effects are *only* observed when TAs work in structured settings with high-quality support and training. Using a TA in an informal, unsupported teaching role could impact negatively on [student] outcomes.

Notice the elements that he highlights:

- Structured settings
- High-quality support
- Training.

These recommendations are based on research conducted over many years, on both sides of the Atlantic, some of which we have already referred to. But what does he mean by *structured settings*? And what is *high-quality support*? A useful way of thinking about that may be to think of the situations that new TAs can find themselves in. In primary schools it may look something like this:

TA (new to the classroom):   *So what can I do to help?*
Teacher: *Oh would you just help Jake with his reading. He's really struggling.*

This is what James Richardson is telling us *not* to do: send the TA off into some corner with a student who is struggling, and expect them to just get on with it and solve the student's problems without any further guidance. Yes, the student will have some attention, from someone who wants to help him, and it will no doubt relate to reading. But teaching reading is a skilled job of work, and the TA may not have the necessary skills. Many primary school teachers who work in Key Stage 2 have limited skills in the teaching of reading, as that is an area more generally associated with Foundation Stage/Phase and KS1. This student is *struggling* with reading so he needs an expert, not just a kindly person who will give him 'tea and sympathy'. Students who have fallen behind – but who are capable of learning – need an accelerated programme of learning. If we are to close the gap and help them catch up with their peers, they need a very specific and focused programme of work which will move them along faster than their peers so that they can catch up. This student has been making slower progress than his peers – hence his being behind – so he needs a reading *expert* to teach him. The TA is not likely to be that expert.

The real problem identified in the research is not that this is the experience of new TAs, but that it is a pattern for so many TAs, including those who are experienced. But 'experienced' does not necessarily equal 'skilled'. Even the experienced TA needs structure and support for her assignments. There is a good deal of research which shows – unsurprisingly – that when TAs are properly trained, they can provide effective support. This research has typically focused on specific programmes that are being introduced in schools. So the TA will be trained to deliver the programme, and will deliver it faithfully, so that the desired improvement is seen in students' performance. This is the sort of *structured setting* and *quality support* that is suggested in James Richardson's recommendations. And the *training* element is obviously present too.

The Education Endowment Foundation (EEF) produced a guidance report in March 2015, *Making Best Use of Teaching Assistants*. Authors Jonathan Sharples, Rob Webster and Peter Blatchford make seven recommendations for good practice. These are aimed at headteachers and members of senior leadership teams and you will find a summary in the nearby box.

Seven recommendations for the best use of Teaching Assistants

TAs in everyday classroom contexts:

1. Avoid using TAs as an 'informal teaching resource for low attaining pupils'.
2. Assign TAs tasks that will 'add value to what teachers do, not replace them'.
3. Ensure that what TAs do will help students develop as independent learners.
4. Prepare TAs fully for their assigned classroom roles.

TAs who deliver structured interventions outside the classroom:

5.   TAs should be used to deliver 'high-quality one-to-one and small group support using structured interventions'.
6.   TAs should use 'evidence-based interventions' when working with groups or individuals.

Linking the work of TAs and teachers:

7.   Make explicit the connections between the learning which occurs during classroom teaching and learning related to structured interventions.

Source: Sharples et al., 2015

But these recommendations can also be applied at classroom level by teachers and SENCOs. There is no need to wait for headteachers and senior leadership to set the parameters for the TA's work. You can:

- Avoid using the TA as an informal teaching resource for low-attaining pupils.
- Use the TA to add value to what you do, rather than replacing you.
- Use your TA to help students develop independence and manage their own learning.
- Ensure your TA is fully prepared for her role in the classroom.
- Use your TA to deliver high-quality, structured, evidence-based interventions, either one-to-one or to small groups.
- Ensure that explicit connections are made between student learning from everyday classroom teaching and learning through structured interventions.

There are a variety of pro formas that have been developed for auditing practice in your school and classroom in relation to TAs. We have already referred to several of them in this book, but you will find further resources in the appendices to allow you to monitor the work of TAs individually (in parallel with appraisal systems used for teachers). We would suggest that you always document the collaborative work you engage in with TAs, building a portfolio of evidence for both teacher and TA that you have engaged in professional development relating to your specific classroom responsibilities and your joint work as members of the same instructional team.

Tensions and solutions

In 2005, Karen Vincett and her colleagues reported on a piece of research which used observation and surveys to investigate collaborative practices between teachers and TAs in UK classrooms. They identified 'tensions' which can prevent or reduce the likelihood of effective collaborations between teachers and TAs:

- TAs' lack of knowledge of effective classroom practices.
- TAs' concerns over their own status.
- Teachers' lack of knowledge of how best to work with TAs.
- Lack of time for teachers and TAs to meet for joint planning.

As a teacher or SENCO, think what you can do to reduce or eliminate these 'tensions' and thus free up teachers and TAs to be more effective in their joint responsibilities for students. We would suggest:

TAs' lack of knowledge can be combatted by training, both in subject area knowledge (if they are to be assigned to faculties or departments) and in pedagogy.

TAs' concerns over their own status can be combatted by clarifying the extent and limits of their roles and responsibilities, but also by clear indications that they are valued, in ways such as those we have suggested here.

Teachers' lack of knowledge of how best to work with TAs can also be combatted by training, on a whole-school or faculty basis. The nasen training materials for SENCOs which are listed in Appendix 1 include a section on *Working with Others,* with slides, worksheets, handouts and an outline for delivering the training, or for providing self-directed professional development.

Lack of time for teachers and TAs to meet for joint planning may need some inventiveness and require significant negotiation skills, but can be combatted by relatively small adjustments to timetables. The larger problem is more likely to be one of entrenched attitudes and resistance to changing long-established (but not necessarily the most efficient) ways of deploying TAs.

All these, we would suggest, are within the reach of teachers and SENCOs who are willing to take on the challenge of improving the effectiveness of TAs.

And so – before giving the last word to a former TA – we wish you well with this new phase in your professional development – adding to your repertoire of teaching skills the practices associated with the collaborative work of supervising the work of TAs. TAs have been an integral part of school life in the past and there is little doubt that they will continue to contribute to our education system well into the future. This book was designed to help you ensure that that future is brighter – for TAs as they develop their own competence and skills, for students as schools deploy and support TAs more effectively, enhancing the impact of their work.

> The 2009 report of the *Lamb Inquiry. Special Educational Needs and Parental Confidence* recommended that TAs may have a variety of useful roles, including: "supporting teachers in classrooms; working with teachers to support a wide range of children in their learning; providing targeted interventions for individuals and small groups of children, under the direction of a teacher, and on programmes and interventions for whichthey have been trained."
>
> However it also specified: "To ensure that children benefit from the support of teaching assistants there has to be a ruthless focus on the impact of how they are deployed and on the skills they need to support children's learning. Underpinning this is a core principle that the teacher takes responsibility for the outcomes of every child, through planning and the monitoring of progress."

The view from the chalkface

Anita Wooltorton

Posted 7 September 2014 at www.tafocus.co.uk

Only now, as I face the first day back at the chalkface, after a blissful few weeks which flitted by all too fitfully, do I feel that I can tackle the subject of what it means to be a TA: I needed that distance because, when you actually consider the statement 'I am a Teaching Assistant', nobody, until fairly recently, has had the vaguest damned idea about just what I was claiming!

Let me explain. A taxi driver drives a taxi, a teacher teaches, but just who or what does a teaching assistant assist; are we there to assist the teach*er* or the teach*ing*, or, as has been the case in the vast majority of positions which fall under the general heading of TA, is neither a better answer?

Most people who came into this profession have found themselves supporting the learning of individual students, sometimes out of the classroom, with most of these students having been encumbered with a statement of special educational needs. The burgeoning growth of TA numbers is pretty consistent with ... the need for inclusion ... and the closure of nasty, expensive special schools which kept these students out of the mainstream: what was an innovation in the 1970s is now a job which employs over 300,000 people in the UK, and has become the accepted norm in just about every school in the country.

However, in the charge towards inclusion, normally quite sane, measured, methodical people in education failed to ask themselves the very questions they expected their teaching staff to ask of their students each and every lesson: *What* are we aiming to achieve by placing TAs within schools? *Who* is the best person for this job? *When* should they be employed? *Why* are they necessary? *Where* should they work? *How* will we measure their achievements?

What we see, as teaching assistants became part of the education framework, are assumptions made in high places that whilst we were deemed necessary, to 'deal with' statemented and other problematic students on a day-to-day basis, little thought was given to the how, what, where, when and why of our employment ... and with the unquestioning acceptance of generations of education ministers and officials, local authority personnel, headteachers, teachers, etc. the cheap, thoughtless, unprofessional misuse of teaching assistants became the status quo.

Hard words? Let me take you back to my first job as a Learning Support Assistant, when my then SENCO informed me that the gentleman in charge of education for my local county council viewed teaching assistants as "a bunch of middle-aged women who sit at the back of the class with the 'numpties' and try to keep them quiet".

His words were totally unprofessional, and politically incorrect, but, you know what? He had a point, because the study by Peter Blatchford et al. found that 'middle-aged women' was what most of us were, and sitting at the back of the class with the most vulnerable students was what most of us were doing. Because none of the 'movers and shakers' in education had asked those important questions, teaching assistants found themselves, over the years, doing anything and everything, from photocopying and general admin, to actively teaching whole classes on virtual slave-labour wages for headteachers who enthusiastically interpreted 'cover supervision' to mean anything that would get them out of a hole, cheaply. But by far the largest group were those of us trailing after statemented students from class to class, in an endless battle to ensure that they 'kept up with the rest'.

Some of us found our way into schools by volunteering to help out with our own kids, and subsequently found that it suited, hours- and holiday- wise, and the money on offer came in handy. As the years went by, this idea of women, locally based, of 'a reasonable standard of education'(!), working hours which suited their commitments (if not their bank balance), became entrenched in education circles, especially as teachers moved further away from the schools they taught in, and moved jobs more frequently to keep pace with increasingly accelerated career paths: we, the support staff, became the stabilising factor, the friendly face of the status quo in schools ... we weren't going anywhere...

And we colluded in this educational sleepwalking, because we are nice people; we wanted to help, to work in education with the vulnerable and less able, to feel a part of something that mattered, and we wouldn't rock the boat, even if we wondered how watching an hour-long film about a kid breaking up a classroom could be called sufficient training on 'behaviour problems and how to deal with them', or how we could work in a Maths department effectively when nobody seemed bothered that we didn't know how the new Maths worked!

Okay, this may not be the same for every TA, but I'm willing to bet that I've struck a few chords with more than a few of you.

However, our past doesn't have to be our future, and it is up to us to push for the changes so badly needed. For example, how can a secondary school attract the right people to work with the most vulnerable and needy students when the headteacher *still* refuses to advertise TA jobs properly, claiming it is an unjustified expense when 'word of mouth' will do? It's like the old vaudeville joke about the bloke applying for a handyman's job who couldn't do anything in that line, but who claimed he qualified as 'handy' because he just lived around the corner!

We, all 300,000 of us, need to get our act together, and drag the reluctant dinosaurs into this century. [If you're a TA] try something for me, will you? Ask about training for your job, and if you want to specialise, see what courses are available in your area, because these courses are for you, and the students you work with deserve the best, not the cheapest, option. If you attend an interview for a school support job, make a point of asking what the school can do for *you*, what are the career prospects, and if they, like the academy sponsor who came to one of my previous schools with glorious plans for the teaching staff, but who stared at me like I'd just hit him in the face with a frozen halibut when I asked him his plans for TA career enhancement, my advice would be to 'run like a bunny in the opposite direction' because "Erm … well … we really do value what teaching assistants do … erm" just ain't good enough anymore!

Ask for specifics; do they want a Teaching Assistant to assist teachers in a certain department working with all (and I mean, all) abilities of student, or do they want Learning Support, trained to work with students with specific problems, or do they want a Learning Mentor, guiding all abilities throughout their school life?

Personally, I will breathe a sigh of relief when I see our profession attracting as many male applicants as women, not simply as a stepping stone into teaching, but as a career choice in its own right. Only then will I forget "middle-aged women sitting with the 'numpties'".

Anita Wooltorton is an experienced TA and union representative. She is old enough to view the world with a very jaundiced eye, expressing those views very loudly without adding "with respect" before she starts speaking, but young enough to want to actually change what she considers to be extremely unfair. The views expressed here are her own personal insight.

Bibliography

DCSF (2009) *Lamb Inquiry. Special Educational Needs and Parental Confidence.* London: DCSF.
Department for Education (2015) *Special Educational Needs and Disability Code of Practice: 0 to 25 Years.* London: DfE. Available at: www.gov.uk/...data/.../SEND_Code_of_Practice_January_2015.pdf (accessed: 20.4.15).
Richardson, J. (2015, 9 March) Deploying teaching assistants effectively: turning evidence into practical recommendations for the classroom. Blog available at: www.nahtedge.org.uk/Newsandviews/BlogListing/TabId/422/PostId/1046/deploying-tas-effectively.aspx (accessed: 20.4.15).

Sharples, J., Webster, R. and Blatchford, P. (2015) *Making Best Use of Teaching Assistants*. London: Education Endowment Foundation.

Versey, J. (2006) Working with teaching assistants to support learning in secondary schools. *Education in Science (EiS)*, 28, 21–3.

Vincett, K., Cremin, H. and Thomas, G. (2005) *Teachers and Teaching Assistants Working Together: A Handbook*. Buckingham: Open University Press.

Watkinson, A. (2008) *Leading and Managing Teaching Assistants. A Practical Guide for School Leaders, Managers, Teachers and Higher-level Teaching Assistants*. Abingdon: Routledge.

Appendix I

Useful websites and other sources of information

The following list contains items that are both *for* Teaching Assistants and *about* Teaching Assistants. Those that have been produced for TAs can be forwarded to your TAs or used as the basis for in-house training.

The Teaching Assistant series produced by Continuum books. Details can be found at: www. bloomsbury.com/uk/series/teaching-assistants-series. This includes topics such as literacy, numeracy, dyslexia, dyspraxia, ADHD, behaviour, with the books written specifically for TAs.

A Whole School Approach to Improving Access, Participation and Achievement. These are materials produced by nasen and intended for SENCOs to provide training to other school staff. The Secondary Training toolkit is available at: www.nasen.org.uk. It includes training notes, activity sheets, information sheets and links to other resources, with one of the four modules relating to *Working with Others*.

Maximising the Impact of Teaching Assistants (MITA) project: www.maximisingtas.co.uk. Information about the MITA project, and other research relating to the work of TAs: *Effective Deployment of TAs* (EDTA), *Making a Statement* (MaST) and *Deployment and Impact of Support Staff* (DISS) can be found on this website, as well as downloadable guidance and pro forma for conducting a school audit on the deployment of TAs.

www.tafocus.co.uk. This website was designed to provide information about TAs but has – not surprisingly – garnered considerable interest from TAs themselves. Here you will find articles and blogs, links to courses for TAs, relevant research and other websites of interest. There is also an associated Facebook page.

www.youtube.com. Clips from the former Teachers TV website are now freely available on YouTube. Especially helpful are John Bayley's clips on various aspects of behaviour, but if you search the website using the term 'Teaching Assistant' you will find a large number of clips produced specifically for TAs.

http://learning.wales.gov.uk/resources/browse-all/observing-children. On this page you will find a downloadable version of the Welsh government publication *Observing Children* referred to in Chapter 4.

http://education.byu.edu/istap. An international website for Teaching Assistants/Education Paraprofessionals/Teacher Aides, with contributions from the United Sates, the UK, Australia and Canada. This website includes factsheets for a variety of special needs/disabilities, information on

© 2016, *Achieving Outstanding Classroom Support in Your Secondary School*, J. Morgan, C. Jones and S. Booth-Coates, Routledge

effective classroom practice, including working in collaboration with teachers, and links to other resources. There is also an associated Facebook page.

Teaching Assistants: Support in Action. This is a free online unit of study, part of the Open University's *Open Learn* materials. Available at: www.open.edu/openlearn/education/educational-technology-and-practice/educational-practice/teaching-assistants-support-action/content-section-0. Content of the unit includes: how the UK's teaching assistant workforce came into being; understanding that TAs are part of a wider assistant workforce in public services; the diverse roles and distinctive contributions of TAs; and skills that TAs use to provide effective support. The course is primarily aimed at TAs, or those who would like to become TAs.

A search using the term 'Teaching Assistant' on the webpage www.theguardian.com/teacher-network/teacher-blog will give you access to a large number of items that have been contributed in recent years, tracking reactions to both research findings and changes in policy/legislation relating to TAs.

www.nrcpara.org is the website of the National Resource Center for Paraprofessionals [TAs] in the United States. The site offers links to individual states where there are initiatives relating to paraprofessionals [TAs], provides information about the annual conference which is held in different locations around the United States each year, and information about training materials and resources, some of which can be downloaded for free. Presentations from the annual conference are uploaded to the website each year and freely accessible.

Michael Giangreco, a researcher at the University of Vermont, has for many years been compiling a database of research relating to TAs/paraprofessionals. Many of the items are available as full-text documents on the website, which can be accessed at: www.uvm.edu/~cdci/?Page=parasupport/chrono.html.

The Evidence for Policy and Practice Information and Co-ordinating Centre (EPPI-Centre) is part of the Social Science Research Unit at the UCL Institute of Education. Available at http://eppi.ioe.ac.uk/cms, a search of the *Education* section of the database using terms such as 'Teaching Assistant', 'Support staff' and 'LSA' will return some 40 items, many of which can be accessed directly through the website.

© 2016, *Achieving Outstanding Classroom Support in Your Secondary School*, J. Morgan, C. Jones and S. Booth-Coates, Routledge

Books for Teaching Assistants

This list is by no means exhaustive, but offers a selection of books which you may wish to purchase as a professional development resource for the TAs in your school. You can of course copy the list for your TAs to make them aware of resources they can purchase themselves.

Arnold, C. and Yeomans, J. (2011) *Psychology for Teaching Assistants*, 2nd edition. Stoke-on-Trent: Trentham Books.

Bentham, S. (2005) *A Teaching Assistant's Guide to Managing Behaviour in the Classroom*. London: Routledge.

Bentham, S. (2011) *A Teaching Assistant's Guide to Child Development and Psychology in the Classroom*, 2nd edition. London: Routledge.

Brookes, G. (2008) *The Complete Guide for Teaching Assistants in Secondary Education*. London: Continuum.

Burnham, L. (2006) *101 Essential Lists for Teaching Assistants*. London: Continuum.

Burnham, L. (2011) *Brilliant Teaching Assistant: What You Need to Know to be a Truly Outstanding Teaching Assistant*. Upper Saddle River, NJ: Prentice Hall.

Canavan, C. (2014) *Supporting Pupils on the Autism Spectrum in Secondary Schools: A Practical Guide for Teaching Assistants*. London: Routledge.

Constable, C. (2013). *Teaching Assistant's Pocketbook*. Alresford: Teachers' Pocketbooks

Cowley, S. (2013) *The Seven T's of Practical Differentiation (Alphabet Sevens)*. CreateSpace Independent Publishing.

Dupree, J. (2006) *Help Students Improve Their Study Skills: A Handbook for Teaching Assistants in Secondary Schools*. London: David Fulton.

Fox, G. (2007) *A Handbook for Learning Support Assistants: Teachers and Assistants Working Together*. Abingdon: Routledge. (ISBN: 1-8431-2081-X)

Graf, M. (2009) *The Teaching Assistant's Guide to Understanding and Supporting Learning*. London: Continuum.

Hryniewicz, L. (2013) *Teaching Assistants: The Complete Handbook*, 3rd edition. Abingdon: Adamson Books.

Lee, C. (2010) *The Complete Guide to Behaviour for Teaching Assistants and Support Staff*. London: Sage.

Parker, M., Lee, C., Gunn, S., Heardman, K., Knight, R.H., Pittman, M., Richards, G. and Armstrong, F. (2007) *Key Issues for Teaching Assistants: Working in Diverse and Inclusive Classrooms*. London: Routledge.

Townsend, M. (2009) *A Toolkit for the Effective Teaching Assistant*, 3rd edition. London: Sage.

Watkinson, A. (2010) *The Essential Guide for New Teaching Assistants: Assisting Learning and Supporting Teaching in the Classroom*. London: Routledge.

Younie, S., Capel S. and Leask, M. (2008) *Supporting Teaching and Learning in Schools: A Handbook for Higher Level Teaching Assistants*. London: Routledge.

© 2016, *Achieving Outstanding Classroom Support in Your Secondary School*, J. Morgan, C. Jones and S. Booth-Coates, Routledge

Top tips
Thinking time

Most students need time to think of answers to your questions. This is particularly true of students with specific learning difficulties, such as dyslexia, or any speech and language difficulties, but thinking time also helps other students who have no recognised difficulties.

No doubt you already use the strategy 'Don't put your hands up straight away – I want you all to think carefully about your answer', so that the speedy (or rash) students are not the only ones called on to answer your questions. But the research suggests that teachers typically wait less than two seconds before taking a response to their questions. It can feel uncomfortable to wait for answers, but you can raise your hand and do a silent 'count-down' with your fingers if that helps you. It will also help the students to see when you are ready to take an answer.

Students who need additional time to process language will need time to process the question before they can think of processing an answer. So you need to be sure to provide plenty of thinking time.

And resist the temptation to repeat or rephrase the question while they are thinking, because that will interrupt the slow-processing student, and he/she will have to start again. Also, if you re-phrase the question, they may well assume you have asked a different question – and start the thinking process all over again.

Here's an illustration to demonstrate the importance of thinking time!

> Imagine your brain is a library. All books and other materials are neatly categorised on shelves, making information easily accessible to us. When we need a particular piece of information we can go to the appropriate shelf and there it is. Pupils (and adults) with Speech Language and Communication Difficulties and other difficulties may not have such a good system. It may be that their library has been 'trashed' and all the books are in a heap in the floor. Think how much harder it then is for them to access information in order to answer questions. They must rummage through the whole pile of books in order to find what they need – it could be anywhere. And if we repeat a question in a different way, they then have to start rummaging through the pile again!

© 2016, *Achieving Outstanding Classroom Support in Your Secondary School*, J. Morgan, C. Jones and S. Booth-Coates, Routledge

Top tips
Types of questions

Low-level questions ask *When? What? Who? How much?* and generally have very specific correct answers. They are referred to as low-level questions because they 'just' require recall and memorisation of facts, and are generally considered necessary preparation for higher-level thinking.

But think for a moment what that implies for the student with poor recall, such as the student with dyslexia. He may not only never get the low-level questions right, but may also be considered incapable of answering higher-level questions which require analysis of the facts (the answers to the low-level questions). How is he ever to developed deeper thinking skills?

When learning outcomes include the development of higher-level thinking, not just analysis of specific facts, we can use the type of open-ended higher-level questions that allows all students to answer – and be correct. Questions such as: *Why do you think...?* or *What do you think happened next?*

The answers you get may not strictly be correct but they do offer all students a chance to answer, and have their ideas considered. Be prepared for some off-the-wall logic, because the most inventive and interesting responses may well come from students you consider to be less able – because they think differently. It can take a while for students to get used to the idea that anything is possible, and that they can answer as well as the next student. But it is worth persisting because it will involve more students in the long run, and allow more students to air their ideas – and be 'right'.

© 2016, *Achieving Outstanding Classroom Support in Your Secondary School*, J. Morgan, C. Jones and S. Booth-Coates, Routledge

Top tips
Meeting the needs of dyslexic learners

Reading

- Avoid asking the student to read aloud unless you are sure they have both the necessary skill level and the confidence.
- Allow students to listen to audio versions of novels before starting a book (if available, or record the text onto a CD; some are available on YouTube).
- Give key vocabulary at the start of each topic.
- Use coloured overlays – experiment to see which colour the student prefers.

Copying from the board

- Avoid if possible (this is a *very difficult* task for a student with dyslexia – give a handout instead).
- Have the student put a different coloured dot at the start of each sentence so tracking is easier.
- Change the background colour of the Interactive Whiteboard (IWB) to off-white – white can be too glaring.
- Mini whiteboards are easier to copy from.
- Following instructions: give short manageable chunks; ask students to repeat instructions back to you to make sure they understand.

Writing

- Show a finished piece of work or an example of the layout so the student can see how to present their work.
- Use a task planner sheet to organise work into steps.
- Use writing frames to help structure what the student wants to say.
- Use word processing whenever possible.
- Offer personalised topic word banks and high-frequency word lists.

Handouts/worksheets

- Use a larger font in Comic Sans, Times New Roman, Century Gothic (seek student preference).
- Highlight important information so they know what to focus on.
- Use a bold font for headings and subheadings.
- Ensure photocopies are clear and easy to read.
- Use pastel coloured paper.
- Don't overcrowd the page.
- Use visuals if possible.

© 2016, *Achieving Outstanding Classroom Support in Your Secondary School*, J. Morgan, C. Jones and S. Booth-Coates, Routledge

Organisation

- Label resources for easier access (use visuals/symbols).
- Cater for different learning styles.
- Provide a prompt card for often repeated procedures, e.g. fair tests in Science.

Mathematics

- Use maths books with larger squares.
- Provide (or have the student make his own) multiplication square.
- Use number lines.
- Use concrete resources as a learning tool, e.g. Dienes blocks.
- Use interactive maths games.
- Worded problems – can they be simplified/broken down into stages?
- Check that students understand the vocabulary.
- Symbols – are students using them correctly?
- Times tables – accept that some may never be learnt – focus on 2, 5 and 10; use a tables square or calculator for others.

Low self-esteem

- Turn mistakes into learning opportunities.
- Keep the learning outcomes the same but differentiate tasks to help the student reach success.
- Overlearning is essential – what they have learned one day they may not remember the next.

Resources

Have resources ready so everything you need is at hand. This could include:

- Highlighters – many dyslexic students have visual strengths and using colour will help them to focus and remember.
- Spare pens/ pencils – not having a pen is a very common work-avoidance strategy.
- Blank cards – to prepare on the spot memory joggers (e.g. key words, phonic rules, number facts, subject vocabulary).
- Mini whiteboard – to simplify and break down instructions, to copy from if the student needs to copy from the board.
- Rewards – merits, stickers, etc.

General tips

- Remember the ultimate goal in supporting dyslexic students is to encourage independent learning. Support as appropriate, challenge sometimes and always have high expectations.
- Make the links for the student, e.g. in History ask, *Did you notice that double 'e' in Queen Victoria?*
- Check you know the objectives for every lesson – this will help you to simplify instructions and break down tasks into manageable steps while ensuring the student is still meeting the learning objectives.
- Support in a multi-sensory way.
- Praise efforts and focus on what has been achieved.
- Scribe for the student if the tasks requires it but ensure the student is focusing and dictating the text (not using this as avoiding work or chatting with friends).

© 2016, *Achieving Outstanding Classroom Support in Your Secondary School*, J. Morgan, C. Jones and S. Booth-Coates, Routledge

Top tips
Speech, language and communication

1. **Check the child's hearing.** Even low levels of hearing loss prevent children hearing the subtleties of language, especially initial consonants and endings of words.

2. **Don't make assumptions.** Speech and language difficulties can be associated with both expressive and receptive language. A student may be articulate (expressive language), but that doesn't necessarily mean she is able to process what you're saying (receptive language).

3. **Modify your language.** You can adjust your vocabulary, the length of your sentences or the speed of delivery.

4. **Chunk instructions.** Avoid giving strings of instructions. Better to have a student respond to one or two successfully, then receive the next instruction.

5. **Observe, observe, observe children.** You can gain a great deal of useful information through careful observation.

6. **Allow extra time to enable children to process information.** All students can benefit from 'wait time' to allow them to think things through thoroughly and at their own pace.

7. **Provide either/or answers.** This allows the student to recognise a correct answer, rather than always having to produce it.

8. **Use visual aids where/whenever possible.** This is general good practice as it allows more students to access more of the curriculum more of the time.

© 2016, *Achieving Outstanding Classroom Support in Your Secondary School*, J. Morgan, C. Jones and S. Booth-Coates, Routledge

Top tips
ASD (Autistic Spectrum Disorders)

1. Make a visual timetable for the child to know exactly what is going to happen and in what order.

2. Provide visual prompts during individual work sessions.

3. Help the child to express his/her feelings using pictorial or visual aids, e.g. feelings fans, traffic lights.

4. Always pre-warn the child of changes that are likely to occur, e.g. a fire alarm, change in staffing, Christmas concert, etc.

5. Be predictable, consistent and reliable.

6. Encourage the wider social circle to adopt the same approaches.

7. Give the child time to process language – wait for a response – and check for understanding.

8. Avoid abstract terms, jokes, figures of speech or sarcasm.

9. Keep instructions as simple as possible.

10. Begin an instruction with the child's name. Individuals with an ASD may not think of themselves as 'Everyone' or 'Class'.

11. Provide opportunities for the transfer of skills; these will not be automatically transferred from one subject to another.

12. Provide alternative activities at break- and lunchtimes. Many individuals find these times very stressful.

13. Transition between lessons – and in particular changing for PE – can also cause anxiety, so make flexible arrangements.

14. Give rewards that are motivational for the individual, e.g. time on the computer or examining a special interest. Conventional rewards such as certificates or stickers can be meaningless to individuals with ASD.

15. Involve home – create a home–school diary.

© 2016, *Achieving Outstanding Classroom Support in Your Secondary School*, J. Morgan, C. Jones and S. Booth-Coates, Routledge

16. Examine the environment for sensory aspects – lighting, seating, smells, textures – that may cause distress.

17. Be sensitive to issues such as lining up or eye contact – close physical proximity and eye contact can be very uncomfortable for students with ASD.

© 2016, *Achieving Outstanding Classroom Support in Your Secondary School*, J. Morgan, C. Jones and S. Booth-Coates, Routledge

Top tips
SEBD (Social, Emotional and Behavioural Disabilities)

1. Make rules and expectations clear, check that children and young people understand how to meet these.

2. Make instructions or requests specific, preface them with the child or group's name, and use phrases such as 'I need you to …, thank you' or 'I want you to …, thanks'.

3. Allow time for compliance by turning away and coming back later to check that they have responded.

4. Use least-intrusive approaches to poor behaviour first – for example, proximity control (moving closer to the inattentive student), proximal praise (praising others who have responded to requests), refocusing a child's attention on the task, or restating rules and expectations – in a calm and positive manner, to the whole class.

5. Do not engage in arguments with students but use techniques such as 'partial agreement', e.g. 'I understand that might be so, but I need you to sit quietly now, thank you.'

6. Give a clear warning before providing a sanction and follow up on it.

7. Rebuild relationships after giving a sanction. Look for and acknowledge more positive behaviour.

8. Use 'I' messages to remind ('I'm disappointed that …') and 'You' messages to encourage ('You know so much about …' 'You make me laugh when…').

9. Do not take poor behaviour personally; calm yourself before responding to behaviour that challenges you.

10. Seek the support of colleagues, ask for positive strategies that others have found useful.

© 2016, *Achieving Outstanding Classroom Support in Your Secondary School*, J. Morgan, C. Jones and S. Booth-Coates, Routledge

Top tips
Working with teenagers

There is plenty of advice available on how to connect with and develop positive relationships with teens. Pat Wolfe (http://patwolfe.com/2011/09/the-adolescent-brain-a-work-in-progress) suggests some ways in which teachers can make the most of teen characteristics.

- Teens don't like to sit and listen for long – so keep presentations short and then have students demonstrate knowledge and understanding through poster presentations, teaching a fellow student, or writing in a journal. Short bursts are more effective than sustained transmission of information.

- They like to argue – so engage them in debate, with real-life issues to discuss, whatever the curriculum area.

- They are digital natives and at ease with technology – so give them research projects that involve the internet and electronic resources, then have them produce multi-media presentations to show their results and understanding.

You will also find advice at the following locations:

- www.ahaparenting.com/ages-stages/teenagers
- www.worldfoodprize.org/.../20_Tips_For_Working_With_Teenagers_3
- http://pearsonclassroomlink.com/articles/1212/1212_0202.htm

© 2016, *Achieving Outstanding Classroom Support in Your Secondary School*, J. Morgan, C. Jones and S. Booth-Coates, Routledge

Top tips
Differentiation

In a March 2012 blog, Edna Sackson lists ten ways to differentiate learning. We have paraphrased them here.

1. **Let go.** Hand some of the responsibility for learning over to the students.

2. **Change your expectations.** Remember that you are teaching individuals, so flexibility of approach is key.

3. **Change the sequence.** Although we do need to consider sequences of skills, it is also good to give students opportunities for demonstrating higher-order skills (prediction, problem-solving) even if you feel they are lacking knowledge of basic facts.

4. **Use technology creatively.** Your students are digital natives – they use technology easily and naturally – but it is also a natural form of differentiation because they will use the technology at the level of their understanding – but they will all use it and will generally engage more willingly in learning activities which involve technology.

5. **Care about what matters to them.** Students will always engage more when they can relate to the topic, so you need to know which topics they are interested in.

6. **Assess *for* learning.** This is the formative assessment that is so valuable in helping you monitor students' understanding and adjusting what you do in response. Almost any activity can provide you with assessment information. It certainly doesn't have to be a formal test.

7. **Embrace inquiry as a stance.** Help your students to understand that asking questions is perfectly acceptable, because that is one of the things that drives an enquiring mind. If we can awaken students' curiosity it is a big step forward for struggling students.

8. **Don't be the only teacher.** Make sure students have opportunities to learn from each other – and to teach you.

9. **Focus on learning, not work.** We cited research in an earlier chapter that suggested TAs tend to focus very much on task completion rather than development of understanding. You may not have control over the activities the students engage in, if they are set by the teacher, but you can prompt students' thinking and extend their learning, by asking them questions that will allow them to figure out answers.

© 2016, *Achieving Outstanding Classroom Support in Your Secondary School*, J. Morgan, C. Jones and S. Booth-Coates, Routledge

10. **Encourage goal setting and reflection.** If students can set their own goals, they will be much more likely to be motivated than if you set goals for them. And of course effective goal-setting includes regular reflection on whether those goals have been reached (or surpassed), why or why not, and what should be the next goal.

Taken from: http://whatedsaid.wordpress.com/tag/learning

© 2016, *Achieving Outstanding Classroom Support in Your Secondary School*, J. Morgan, C. Jones and S. Booth-Coates, Routledge

Pro forma for feedback from TA

Lesson	Date/Time
TA	Year group/pupils supported
Teacher	

Activity

Comments (if appropriate, include reference to individual students' IEP targets)

© 2016, *Achieving Outstanding Classroom Support in Your Secondary School*, J. Morgan, C. Jones and S. Booth-Coates, Routledge

Index